NOTRE DAME COLLEGE OF EDUCATION
MOUNT PLEASANT
LIVERPOOL L3 5SP

WILLIAM MORRIS
and his world

IAN BRADLEY

WILLIAM MORRIS
and his world

with 145 illustrations

THAMES AND HUDSON

Frontispiece: Morris photographed by
Frederick Hollyer in 1889.

*Printed in Great Britain
by Jarrold & Sons Ltd, Norwich*

WILLIAM MORRIS owed a lot to the forces of capitalism against which he was to engage in 'holy warfare' for most of his life. Without his own comfortable middle-class upbringing, and the £900 annual income which he inherited at the age of twenty-one, it is doubtful if he could ever have embarked on his hazardous career as designer, poet and revolutionary.

The Morrises were a solid and respectable bourgeois family. William Morris senior was a partner in a firm of discount brokers. In 1833, the year before William's birth, he and his wife left their rooms above the office in the City of London and took up residence in Walthamstow, then a quiet village overlooking the Lea Valley and set on the edge of Epping Forest. Morris later wrote, 'We lived in the ordinary bourgeois style of comfort; and since we belonged to the evangelical section of the English Church, I was brought up in what I should call rich establishmentarian puritanism; a religion which even as a boy I never took to.'

William Morris was the third of nine children, all but two of whom went on to lead conventional Victorian middle-class lives. His eldest sister, Emma, married a Derbyshire clergyman and assisted him in evangelistic work among the local miners. The next child, Henrietta, became a Roman Catholic after visiting Rome with her mother, and never married. The youngest, Alice, married a Devonshire banker. The other sister, Isabella, took a less conventional path when she trained as a nurse at Guy's Hospital in middle age after the death of her husband. She spent the last twenty years of her life working in the slums of south London and became Superintendent of the Rochester and Southwark Mission.

Of William's brothers, Hugh, the eldest, became a gentleman farmer in Hampshire, Thomas joined the Gordon Highlanders, and Arthur served in India and China with the 60th Royal Rifles. The fourth, Edgar, lived in Herefordshire off his capital until it ran out, and then went to work as a dyer at William's factory at Merton Abbey. A visitor to the works in 1892 reported, 'he is quite happy there, dipping wool all day in the vats, in a shed open on to the garden'.

William Morris seems to have had very little contact with his brothers and sisters, either as a child or in later life. The only one taken

Elm House, Walthamstow, where William Morris was born on 24 March 1834.

into his confidence was Emma, to whom he sent copies of many of the poems he wrote as a young man. He was a solitary child, and never really felt at home with his family's strict religious code.

As a result of William Morris senior's successful speculation in the shares of a Devonshire copper-mine, the family moved from a position of comfortable well-being to one of considerable prosperity. He had bought 272 shares in the mine for £1 each. Their value rapidly rose to £800 each, so that his total holding became worth around £200,000. It was these shares that were to provide his son William with an annual income of £900 when he came of age. More immediately, they enabled the family to move further into the country. In 1840 the Morrises took up residence in Woodford Hall, a Palladian mansion standing in its own park of fifty acres and surrounded on all sides by Epping Forest.

It was in these gracious surroundings that William Morris grew up and developed the love of nature which was to dominate his art and his approach to life. An early weakness in his constitution, which was treated with a diet of calves' foot jelly and beef tea, was soon overcome by hearty walks through the forest. Morris was fascinated by the flora and fauna in the woods, and especially by the dense hornbeam thickets which are a feature of Epping Forest. He had his own garden at Woodford Hall where he spent many hours tending his plants. This love of nature never left him. In his designs for wallpapers and tapestries he used again and again the forms of flower, leaf and bird which he remembered from his rambles through the forest as a boy. In *News From Nowhere*, the Utopian romance which Morris wrote towards the end of his life, England is described as a single beautiful garden.

Morris developed another love in his childhood which remained with him for the rest of his life. This was a passion for all things medieval. Life at Woodford Hall in many ways followed the routine of a manor-house in the Middle Ages. The household brewed its own beer, baked its bread and made butter. There was a meal at high prime, midway between breakfast and dinner, at which the children had cakes, cheese and ale. Morris's father seems to have been an enthusiast for the Middle Ages. In 1843 he obtained for himself a coat of arms which included a horse's head. Young William was soon clad in a suit of armour and riding his pony through the forest as a knight of the white horse. In more serious moments he enjoyed exploring the local Essex churches and was particularly struck by their fine brasses. When he was eight his father took him to see Canterbury Cathedral. The details of its Gothic splendour remained imprinted on his mind for a long time. So did the 'room hung with faded greenery' which he saw on a visit to Queen Elizabeth I's hunting lodge at Chingford Hatch in the middle of Epping Forest.

The tomb of William Morris senior in Woodford churchyard with his coat of arms, a horse's head between three horseshoes.

Woodford Hall, the Palladian mansion in Epping Forest where the Morris family lived from 1840 to 1848. Morris's father drove daily to the City by coach and he rode to preparatory school in Walthamstow on a pony.

Queen Elizabeth I's hunting lodge at Chingford Hatch, a favourite childhood haunt of Morris. One of its rooms set the pattern for many of his later decorations.

William's education followed the conventional middle-class pattern. After preparatory school in Walthamstow, he went on to public school, Marlborough, in 1848. Although he had early proved himself to be a voracious reader, devouring all of Sir Walter Scott's Waverley Novels by the time he was nine, William showed more interest at school in outdoor pursuits than in his studies. Endowed with formidable energy and physical strength, he excelled at the sport of singlestick, a form of fencing with a basket-hilted sword. Many of his afternoons at Marlborough were spent in solitary rambles through the Savernake Forest, 'making up stories about knights and faeries'. He also pursued his interest in old buildings. By the time he left Marlborough he had read all the books on architecture and archaeology in the school library and had visited most of the important churches in Wiltshire as well as the ancient British sites at Avebury and Silbury Hill.

A riot by the boys in November 1851 cut short William's time at Marlborough. He was removed by his mother to complete his education with a private tutor at Water House, a Georgian mansion in Walthamshow which had become the new family home following the death of his father in 1848. In the summer of 1852 he gained a place at Exeter College, Oxford. His family confidently expected that this would lead to a career in the Church. Morris probably thought so as well. At Marlborough he had come under the influence of the High Church Oxford Movement which had been inaugurated in the early 1830s by John Henry Newman, John Keble and Edward Pusey. He was powerfully attracted by the piety of the Tractarians and by their

A caricature of Morris revisiting Avebury stone circle with Edward Burne-Jones, probably in June 1874, when they were inspecting Marlborough College with a view to sending Philip Burne-Jones there.

Marlborough College, founded in 1843 principally for the sons of country clergymen.

stress on both the liturgical ceremonial and the social responsibilities of the Church. Where better to go as a preparation for taking Holy Orders than to the home of the Oxford Movement?

Within a few days of going up to Oxford in January 1853, Morris had fallen in love with the city, which was still largely medieval in appearance. He had also met a fellow freshman at Exeter College, Edward Burne-Jones, the son of a Birmingham picture-framer, who was to become his closest friend and companion for the rest of his life. The two men took to each other immediately. They went on daily walks together and had adjacent rooms in the college in their second year. Burne-Jones introduced Morris to other undergraduates who had been at school with him in Birmingham, Richard Dixon, Charles James Faulkner and William Fulford. Before long they were all meeting together in Faulkner's rooms in Pembroke College and talking far into the night. Morris did most of the talking. Burne-Jones recalled one occasion when he 'came tumbling in and talked for the

Oxford High Street in 1860. The city, described by Matthew Arnold as 'whispering from her towers the last enchantments of the Middle Age', made an immediate and lasting impression on Morris, and it was at Oxford that his most enduring friendships were formed.

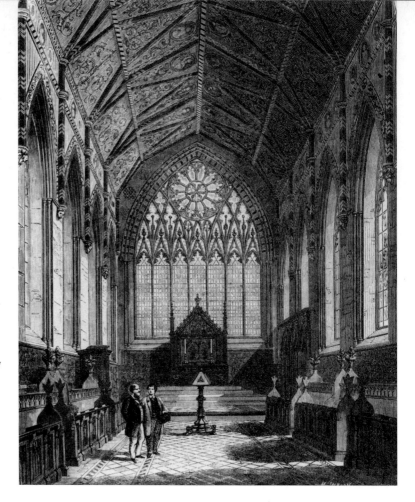

Merton College Chapel, Oxford. Burne-Jones wrote, 'it had been lately renovated by Butterfield, and Pollen, a former Fellow of Merton, had painted the roof of it. Many an afternoon we spent in that chapel. Indeed, I think the buildings of Merton and the cloisters of New College were our chief shrines in Oxford.'

next seven hours or longer'. The others were happy to listen to him, for they regarded him as an attractive and uplifting companion. Dixon later recalled, 'At this time Morris was an aristocrat and a High Churchman. His manners and tastes and sympathies were all aristocratic. His countenance was beautiful in features and expression, particularly in the expression of purity.'

At first, the conversation at these undergraduate gatherings was mostly on theological and ecclesiastical topics. All five young men expected to go into the Church, although in the event only Dixon and Fulford did so, and they were all keen Anglo-Catholics. They also shared a love of poetry, and in particular of Tennyson's Arthurian Legends, which soon supplanted theology as their main topic of conversation. From reading the Oxford Movement's *Tracts for the Times*, they moved to a 'rapid and prodigious assimilation of medieval chronicles and romances'. Morris began his lifelong practice of declaiming verse in a sing-song voice, often for hours at a time. The five undergraduates became a self-conscious literary set. 'The bond', Dixon later recalled, 'was poetry and indefinite literary and artistic inspiration: but not of a selfish character, or rather, not of a self-seeking character. We all had the notion of doing great things for man: in our own way, however: according to our own will and bent.'

This eagerness to embark on an altruistic crusade was largely inspired by three recently published books, each of which had an important effect on Morris's development. Thomas Carlyle's *Past and Present*, published in 1843, contrasted the humane and peaceful world of a twelfth-century monastery with the cruelty and tumult of the nineteenth century. John Ruskin's *The Stones of Venice*, published in 1853, extolled the medieval ideal of craftsmanship in which men found utter satisfaction and ultimate salvation in their work. Charlotte Yonge's *The Heir of Redclyffe*, published in the same year, told of the exploits of a latter-day knight who embodied the chivalric ideals of the Middle Ages. Common to these three books was a eulogy of medieval society, with its high ideals and religious principles, its basis in co-operation rather than competition, and its absence of industrial exploitation and drudgery. Not surprisingly, they fired Morris and his undergraduate friends with a determination to recreate for themselves the atmosphere of the Middle Ages.

The Victorian cult of medievalism, of which Morris became a passionate adherent, was far more than a mere romantic longing for a far-off golden age. It derived from the first serious scholarly exploration in Britain of the literature and society of the Middle Ages. The formation of the Camden Society to provide authoritative medieval texts – from one of which, *The Chronicle of Jocelin of Brakelond*, Carlyle took the story of Abbot Samson and the monastery of St Edmundsbury for *Past and Present*, the foundation of the Chaucer Society and the Early English Text Society, and the inauguration of the Rolls series of early legal enactments, all took place in the mid-nineteenth century. They were manifestations of a growing interest in philology and the derivation of the English language, which culminated in the publication of *The Oxford English Dictionary* in 1858. There was a parallel interest in the origins of English law and society, which found expression in such works as William Stubbs's *Constitutional History of England to 1485*, the first volume of which was published in 1874.

The new knowledge and material on the Middle Ages available to the Victorians as a result of all this scholarship was used and interpreted in many different ways. Tennyson took Sir Thomas Malory's *Morte d'Arthur* as the inspiration for some of his most important poems. Disraeli sought in the Young England Movement to recreate the medieval alliance of nobles and peasants and use it against factory-owners and capitalists. Carlyle and Ruskin used the newly discovered evidence of conditions of life in the Middle Ages to

John Ruskin (1819–1900). Morris described his book *The Stones of Venice* as 'one of the very few necessary and inevitable utterances of the century'.

CHRONICA

JOCELINI DE BRAKELONDA,

DE REBUS GESTIS

SAMSONIS

ABBATIS MONASTERII SANCTI EDMUNDI.

NUNC PRIMUM TYPIS MANDATA

CURANTE

JOHANNE GAGE ROKEWODE.

LONDINI:
SUMPTIBUS SOCIETATIS CAMDENENSIS.
M.DCCC.XL.

An aspect of Victorian medievalism: the Camden Society's 1840 reprint of *The Chronicle of Jocelin of Brakelond*, on which Carlyle based *Past and Present*.

cast serious doubts on the Victorian gospel of progress and to suggest that people might not, in fact, be better off in all respects in the nineteenth century than in all earlier periods. Charlotte Yonge called for a revival of chivalry and knightly virtues. For others it was the monastic ideal and the sense of brotherhood that provided inspiration. A few years before Morris went up to Oxford, John Newman had founded a simple and austere religious community in the village of Littlemore, just outside the city. G.E. Street, the High Church architect, wanted to establish a communal institution for students of religion and art. A similar community had been set up by painters in Rome in the early years of the century.

It was the communal aspect of medieval life which most appealed to Morris and his friends at Oxford. 'I have set my heart on our founding a Brotherhood,' Burne-Jones wrote in May 1853 to a school friend who was about to come up to Oxford, 'Learn "Sir Galahad" by heart: he is to be the patron of our order.' At first, the Brotherhood, as the group now took to calling themselves, seems to have been conceived principally as a religious body, although it was also designed to embody the virtues of medieval chivalry as described in *The Heir of Redclyffe*. Early in 1854, when both he and Morris were seriously considering becoming Roman Catholics, Burne-Jones described its purpose as being to undertake 'this crusade and Holy Warfare against the age'. But before long, the two leading members of the Brotherhood had abandoned religion and dedicated themselves to secular aims.

It was art that diverted Burne-Jones and Morris from their early religious leanings and ended any possibility there might ever have been of their Brotherhood becoming a monastic community. A visit to Belgium and northern France in the summer of 1854 introduced Morris to the splendours of Flemish painting and Gothic architecture. At the same time he read in Ruskin's Edinburgh Lectures of another Brotherhood, calling themselves the Pre-Raphaelites, who painted in the style of the medieval masters. Burne-Jones later recalled:

I was reading in my room when Morris ran in one morning bringing the newly published book with him: so everything was put aside until he read it all through to me. And there we first saw about the Pre-Raphaelites, and there I first saw the name of Rossetti. So many a day after that we talked of little else but paintings which we had never seen.

Millais' *The Return of the Dove to the Ark* (1851), the first Pre-Raphaelite painting that Morris and Burne-Jones saw. It was on view in a shop in Oxford High Street in 1854. 'And then', wrote Burne-Jones, 'we knew.'

The fact that contemporary artists were recreating the art of the Middle Ages acted as an incentive to Morris and Burne-Jones to do the same. In the summer of 1855 they accompanied Fulford on a tour of northern France which took in twenty-four major churches and nine cathedrals, including Chartres, Amiens and Rouen. At the end of this tour, as they were walking along the quayside at Le Havre, Morris and Burne-Jones decided to renounce their intention of taking Holy Orders and instead devote themselves to art.

Morris's decision to embark on an artistic career saddened and shocked his mother, who had regarded the Church as the natural sequel to his time at Oxford. He wrote her a long letter in an effort to persuade her that the family's money had not been wasted on his University education:

A University education fits a man about as much for being a ship-captain as a Pastor of souls. Your money has by no means been thrown away. If the love of friends faithful and true, friends first seen and loved here, if this love is something priceless, and not to be bought again anywhere and by any means; if moreover by living here and seeing evil and sin in its foulest and coarsest forms, as one does day by day, I have learned to hate any form of sin, and to wish to fight against it, is not this well too?

In deciding to devote himself to art, Morris was turning his back on the active participation in social reform towards which his undergraduate reading and thinking had been encouraging him.

A characteristic painting by the leader of the Pre-Raphaelites: Rossetti's *Mary Magdalene at the Door of Simon the Pharisee* (1858). Burne-Jones was the model for Christ.

My dear Mother —

I am almost afraid you thought
me scarcely in earnest when I told you
a month or two ago that I did not intend
taking Holy orders; if this is the case I am
afraid also that my letter now may bore
you, but if you have really made up
your mind that I was in earnest I think
you will be pleased with my resolution.
You said then you remember and said
very truly, that it was an evil thing
to be an idle, objectless man; I am
fully determined not to incur this reproach,
I was so then though I did not tell you
at the time all I thought of,
partly because I had not thought about
it enough myself, and partly because I
wished to give you time to become reconciled
to the idea of my continuing a lay person

Looking back much later on his years at Oxford, Morris recalled that he had been strongly influenced by the writings of Carlyle, Ruskin and Kingsley, all of them vigorous critics of contemporary society and, in the case of the last two, ardent advocates of socialism. 'From them,' he wrote, 'I got into my head some socio-political ideas which would have developed probably but for the attractions of art and poetry.' It was to be thirty years before Morris returned to these ideas, and took up again the youthful interest in social reform that he had abandoned for the sake of art.

While Burne-Jones decided to become a painter, Morris opted for a career as an architect. He had been interested in buildings since childhood, and had subscribed regularly to *The Builder* while an undergraduate. So, after graduating from Oxford, he had himself apprenticed to G. E. Street, with whom he started work in January 1856. Street appealed to Morris as a fellow-medievalist as well as an accomplished architect with a considerable reputation; he was later to design the Law Courts in the Strand, London. There was also the added advantage that his office was in Oxford, so Morris could continue to live in the city he loved and maintain close links with his undergraduate friends. The atmosphere in Street's office was lively and friendly. Because one of the young apprentices had a bad stutter and was better able to sing than to speak, the others developed the habit of chanting to each other in Gregorian plainsong through rolls of foolscap. Morris struck up a particularly close friendship with Street's chief assistant, Philip Webb, who described him quaintly as 'a slim boy like a wonderful bird just out of his shell'.

During 1856 Morris contributed regularly to *The Oxford and Cambridge Magazine*, a monthly review which was started by the Brotherhood at the beginning of the year. He was originally appointed to be its editor, but he handed this task over to Fulford after the first issue. The magazine ran for only twelve months. It was written almost entirely by members of Morris's circle at Oxford. His own contributions included articles on Amiens Cathedral, two chivalric prose romances and several poems, none of them very distinguished. Morris found no difficulty in turning out large quantities of verse that earned the praise of his contemporaries. When Dixon praised his first undergraduate poem, 'The Willow and the Red Cliff', he commented, 'Well, if this is poetry, it is very easy to write', and thereafter he composed a new poem almost daily.

Morris did not stick to architecture for long. He did not enjoy the work on which Street had put him of copying a detailed drawing of the doorway of St Augustine's Church, Canterbury. Early in 1856 Burne-Jones had gone to London to paint under the guidance of the leader of the Pre-Raphaelites, Dante Gabriel Rossetti. Morris visited him every weekend, and soon fell under the Pre-Raphaelite spell,

Opposite, the letter Morris sent to his mother in November 1855 to tell her that he intended to devote himself to an artistic career, and not take Holy Orders as she had hoped. At the end of the letter, he wrote, 'I will by no means give up things I have thought of for the bettering of the world in so far as lies in me.'

Three leading Pre-Raphaelites: (*above*) Ford Madox Brown, sketched by Rossetti; (*below*) Edward Burne-Jones, sketched by Simeon Solomon; (*below right*) Dante Gabriel Rossetti, a self-portrait.

meeting Rossetti, Ford Madox Brown and William Holman Hunt. When Street moved his office to London in the summer, Morris shared lodgings with Burne-Jones, first in Bloomsbury and then in Rossetti's old rooms in Red Lion Square. In July he noted in his diary, 'Rossetti says I ought to paint, he says I shall be able; now as he is a very great man, and speaks with authority and not as the scribes, I must try.' By the end of the year Morris had abandoned the idea of becoming an architect and was learning how to paint with the Pre-Raphaelite master as his tutor.

Rossetti exercised a profound influence on all those artists who came into contact with him. They worshipped him as the founder and leading exponent of the Pre-Raphaelite school of painting which sought to restore and continue the style of art of the Middle Ages before the Renaissance had made it academic and classical. Burne-Jones described him as a man who could 'lead armies or destroy empires if he liked'. For his part, Rossetti desperately needed the support of a small circle of sycophantic followers. For all his youthful gaiety and charm, he was very insecure, as his later lapse into deep melancholy and depression was to show.

Morris regarded Rossetti simply as 'a very great man'. He was all too ready to fall under his influence, commenting to Burne-Jones, 'I want to imitate Gabriel as much as I can'. Some of Morris's biographers have blamed Rossetti for destroying his interest in contemporary problems, and hindering his socialist awakening by instilling into him

William Morris, aged 23. Burne-Jones wrote, 'He was slight in figure in those days; his hair was dark brown and very thick, his nose straight, his eyes hazel-coloured, his mouth exceedingly delicate and beautiful.'

Caricature by Burne-Jones of the studio in Red Lion Square. He shows himself looking at a chair designed by Morris and decorated by Rossetti.

an all-powerful medievalism and a philosophy of art for art's sake. To a certain extent, this was the case. In July 1856, when he had decided at Rossetti's instigation to give up architecture and turn to painting, he wrote: 'I can't enter into politico-social subjects with any interest, for on the whole I see that things are in a muddle, and I have no power or vocation to set them right in ever so little a degree.' But Morris had already turned his back on contemporary problems by his decision to devote himself to art at the end of his second French tour, and he was powerfully affected by medievalism long before he met Rossetti.

Rossetti's great contribution to Morris's artistic development was, quite simply, the discovery and encouragement of his talents. 'If a man has any poetry in him', he had told Morris, 'he should paint, for it has all been said and written, and they have scarcely begun to paint it.' Without this advice, Morris might never have become a designer.

Morris did not shine as a painter. He laboured conscientiously under Rossetti's guidance, but he failed to produce work of any merit. The main reason for this was almost certainly his inability to paint or draw figures. This remained a handicap throughout his life; the animals on Morris's wallpapers were almost all done by Webb, and the human figures in his tapestries by Burne-Jones. Morris soon realized that his talents were better suited to other art-forms. He experimented with stained glass, manuscript illumination and embroidery. Unable to find any suitable furniture for the rooms in Red Lion Square, he designed a huge settle, as well as a table and chairs. 'Morris is rather doing the magnificent there,' Rossetti wrote to a friend, 'and is having some intensely medieval furniture made – tables and chairs like incubi and succubi. He and I have painted the back of a chair with figures

Morris's fresco on the wall of the Oxford Union Debating Hall (now the library). Despite several attempts at restoration, the frescoes have almost completely disappeared.

Opposite, the *Orchard* tapestry (1890) designed by Morris with figures by Burne-Jones. Morris was never good at drawing or painting figures and he generally left a blank outline in his backgrounds to be filled in by other artists (*opposite, below*).

and inscriptions in gules and vert and azure, and we are all three going to cover a cabinet with pictures.' Here, perhaps, was the origin of Morris's lifelong interest in the decorative and useful arts.

There was one important Pre-Raphaelite painting venture, however, in which Morris did take part. In the summer of 1857 Rossetti assembled a group of artists, including Morris and Burne-Jones, to paint frescoes on the walls of the Debating Hall which had just been built for the Oxford Union Society by Benjamin Woodward. The eight bays above the gallery were to be covered with scenes from Malory's *Morte d'Arthur*, which Rossetti regarded as the greatest book in the world apart from the Bible. Morris completed his picture, of Palomydes and La Belle Iseult, before anyone else had finished theirs, and promptly set about painting heraldic beasts and birds on the roof. Unfortunately, the brickwork on which the frescoes were painted had not been damp-proofed, and was covered only by a thin layer of whitewash, with the result that the paint either sank in or flaked off. Further damage was done by smoke and heat from the naked gas-jets which lit the hall, and after only twelve months the frescoes were indecipherable. So they have remained ever since, although Morris repainted the roof in 1875, and there have been several subsequent attempts at restoration.

The atmosphere surrounding the painting of the Oxford Union frescoes was one of youthful high spirits and practical joking. There was none of the rather precious affectation and effeminacy which is sometimes associated with the Pre-Raphaelites. The sound most often heard in the Union Debating Hall while the artists were at work was not the soulful sighing of aesthetes but the fizzing of soda-water bottles

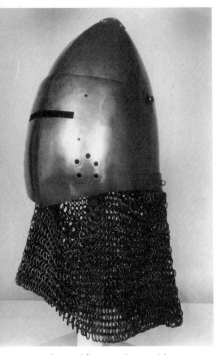

The steel basinet designed by Morris to help him model the armour for his fresco at the Oxford Union.

A cartoon by Max Beerbohm of 'Topsy and Ned settled on the settle in Red Lion Square'. The settle, one of the very few pieces of furniture designed by Morris, was later moved to Red House where it can be seen today.

and the clanking of the suit of armour which Morris had designed and commissioned from a local blacksmith for modelling purposes. Burne-Jones remembered, 'One afternoon when I was working high up at my picture, I heard a strange bellowing in the building, and turning round to find the cause, saw an unwonted sight. The basinet was being tried on, but the visor, for some reason, would not lift, and I saw Morris embedded in iron, dancing with rage and roaring inside. The mail coat came in due time, and was so satisfactory to its designer that the first day it came he chose to dine in it.' This sense of fun and frivolity was shared by all the artists who worked on the Oxford Union frescoes. It even affected Algernon Swinburne, the young Balliol undergraduate who came to watch them, and who was to become the darling of the Late Victorian Aesthetic Movement. None was keener than he on the wild games of bridge and riotous parties with the 'stunners', as the Pre-Raphaelites called the local girls, which followed the long day's work on the frescoes.

The same hearty and convivial atmosphere prevailed in Morris's and Burne-Jones's rooms in Red Lion Square. There were constant practical jokes, such as buckets balanced on the tops of doors and parcels with no contents and accompanied by indecipherable letters sent to favourite enemies. Morris's efforts at furniture-design caused considerable amusement. 'There were many scenes with the carpenter,' Burne-Jones recalled, 'especially I remember the night when the settle came home. We were out when it reached the house, but when we

came in, all the passages and the staircase were choked with vast blocks of timber, and there was a scene. I think the measurements had perhaps been given a little wrongly, and that it was bigger altogether than he had ever meant, but set up it was finally, and our studio was one third less in size.' Red Lion Mary, the easy-going and patient maid who looked after Morris and Burne-Jones, struggled to accommodate their endless stream of visitors, cheerfully spreading mattresses on the floor for friends who stayed there, and when there were no more mattresses, building up beds with books and portmanteaux.

The spirit of Red Lion Square is nicely caught in a description by Val Prinsep, one of Rossetti's pupils, of an evening spent with Morris, Burne-Jones and Rossetti during the painting of the Oxford Union frescoes:

When dinner was over, Rossetti, humming to himself as was his wont, rose from the table and proceeded to curl himself upon the sofa. 'Top', he said, 'read us one of your grinds.' 'No, Gabriel,' answered Morris, 'you have heard them all.' 'Never mind,' said Rossetti, 'here's Prinsep who has never heard them, and besides, they are devilish good.' 'Very well, old chap,' growled Morris, and having got his book he began to read in a sing-song chant some of the poems afterwards published in his first volume. All the time, he was jigging about nervously with his watch chain. . . . I can still recall the scene: Rossetti on the sofa with large melancholy eyes fixed on Morris, the poet at the table reading and ever fidgeting with his watch chain, and Burne-Jones working at a pen-and-ink drawing.

Algernon Charles Swinburne (1837–1909), Pre-Raphaelite poet and aesthete. He left Oxford in 1860 without a degree.

MR MORRIS reading poems to MR BURNE JONES

Caricature by Burne-Jones entitled 'Mr Morris reading poems to Mr Burne-Jones'. Morris frequently read out lengthy extracts from his latest poems to his long-suffering friends.

Three heavy dragoons adopting medieval postures in the original 1881 production of *Patience*, Gilbert and Sullivan's take-off of the Aesthetic Movement.

Opposite, Jane Burden, aged 18, sketched by Rossetti. Henry James wrote, 'It's hard to say whether she's a grand synthesis of all the Pre-Raphaelite pictures ever made – or they a "keen analysis" of her.'

It was undoubtedly an arty atmosphere, and certainly a Bohemian one – for a long time an owl perched in the corner of the main room. But it was anything but effete.

Morris himself was no namby-pamby aesthete of the kind satirized so brilliantly in Gilbert and Sullivan's *Patience*. It is impossible to imagine him, like Reginald Bunthorne, walking down Piccadilly with a poppy or a lily in his medieval hand. He positively exuded an air of heartiness and shunned sentimentality, as in the rhyme which he delighted in reciting:

> *I sits with my feet in a brook,*
> *And if anyone asks me for why,*
> *I hits him a crock with my crook,*
> *For it's sentiment kills me, says I.*

His appearance was rough and even forbidding. After leaving University he never again touched a razor nor visited a barber. As a result, he had a long, shaggy beard and an unkempt mane of curly black hair which was so strong that he encouraged girls to hold on to it while he pulled them up. It was this which gave him his nickname, Topsy, and which caused him to be mistaken for a sea captain and, on one occasion, for a burglar. Morris's clothes were always dishevelled and often torn. They fitted with difficulty round his increasingly corpulent body. In his behaviour he was often clumsy. One of his contemporaries recalled that 'he tumbled about his friends' rooms with a curious aptitude for knocking things over'.

These were hardly characteristics normally associated with a poet. Yet it was as a poet that Morris first came to the notice of the public. In March 1858, just as work was finally being abandoned on the Union frescoes, his first volume of poetry, *The Defence of Guenevere*, was published. The subjects in this collection were all medieval, and were mostly taken from the *Morte d'Arthur*. The language of the poems is archaic and simple, although they show an original use of abrupt broken rhythms. Public reaction to the book was not good. Less than three hundred copies were sold. The *Spectator* reviewer criticized the poems for their 'prosaic baldness', while another critic described them as 'unmanly, effeminate, mystical, affected and obscure'. Morris didn't care very much what they said, for he was in love.

One evening in the autumn of 1857 Rossetti and Burne-Jones had been much struck by the appearance of a girl sitting in the row behind them in the theatre at Oxford. She had a pale face, a long, finely structured neck, and black crinkly hair; the perfect Pre-Raphaelite features, in fact. The girl, who was called Jane Burden, turned out to be the daughter of an Oxford stable-hand. Rossetti asked her to come to model for the paintings at the Union. He was captivated by her, and determined that she should remain within his circle, although he

himself was already in love with another Pre-Raphaelite beauty, Elizabeth Siddal, whom he was to marry three years later. Without any prompting from Rossetti, Morris became infatuated with Jane. He made her the subject of an oil painting, *Queen Guenevere*, and idolized her in one of the better poems in *The Defence of Guenevere*, 'Praise of My Lady':

> *My lady seems of ivory*
> *Forehead, straight nose, and cheeks that be*
> *Hollow'd a little mournfully;*
> Beata mea Domina!

William Morris and Jane Burden became engaged in 1858. Initially, she had not been very enthusiastic about his method of courting, which consisted largely of lengthy readings to her from Dickens's *Barnaby Rudge*. Rossetti seems to have persuaded her that she would enjoy marriage to Morris. In fact, their relationship was to prove disastrous. The trouble was that Morris worshipped Jane as a remote and romanticized ideal. He found it easy to idolize her in paintings or verse as Guenevere, Iseult, or Beatrice, but impossible to treat her in real life as the ordinary working-class girl that she was. Swinburne was right in saying that he should have been content 'to have that wonderful and most perfect stunner of his to look at and

Elizabeth Siddal, sketched by Rossetti. She was married to him for two years and then committed suicide.

Caricature by Rossetti of Morris presenting an engagement ring to Jane Burden.

Opposite, William Morris's only surviving oil painting, *Queen Guenevere* or *La Belle Iseult* (1858). Jane was the model and the painting was retouched and finished by Morris's friends. He is said to have scrawled on the back, 'I cannot paint you, but I love you'.

Charles Faulkner, an undergraduate friend of Morris and one of the founder members of Morris, Marshall, Faulkner & Co. Morris said, 'he had great natural skill with the executive side of art'.

speak to. The idea of marrying her is insane. To kiss her feet is the utmost a man should think of doing.'

Jane, for her part, came to adopt the distant, melancholy role in which Morris and the other Pre-Raphaelites cast her in their verse and paintings. She was neither physically nor emotionally robust, and she was unable to cope with the treatment she received from her fiery tempered husband, who would fling his dinner out of the window if he did not like it. She avoided the utter desperation of Elizabeth Siddal, who was similarly at once idealized and ignored by the Pre-Raphaelite circle, and who took her own life with an overdose of laudanum after only two years of marriage to Rossetti. But from the mid 1860s she was seldom free from illness, and she became increasingly moody and withdrawn.

William and Jane were married in April 1859 at St Michael's Church in Oxford. He was twenty-five and she eighteen. Richard Dixon, who had by now taken Holy Orders, officiated, and inadvertently referred to the couple throughout the service as William and Mary. Charles Faulkner was best man and Burne-Jones was one of the few guests. It was the last gathering of the Brotherhood in Oxford, and it closed a chapter in Morris's life. He would soon be exchanging the squalor and disorder of the bachelor quarters in Red Lion Square for the domestic comforts of a proper home and married life. During a rowing holiday on the Seine the previous summer he had asked Philip Webb to design a house to be built on the meadow which he had bought near the village of Upton in north-west Kent. Webb left Street's office largely on the strength of this commission, and set to work to satisfy Morris's request for a home 'very medieval in spirit'.

Red House, which now stands in the middle of the south London suburb of Bexleyheath, is often regarded as a landmark in the development of English domestic architecture. To Morris it was quintessentially medieval. It went back to the vernacular style of the Cotswold cottage in reaction against the prevailing classical style with its fussy embellishments. The most significant feature of the house was its simplicity. It used ordinary, unadorned red bricks rather than expensive stone or heavy stucco. Form was more important than decoration. Outside it followed the English vernacular tradition with its steeply tiled roofs, long ridge-lines, tall chimney-stacks and deeply recessed porches. Inside it had plain tiled floors, a simple open staircase and large wooden dressers. Red House brought traditional Gothic features into domestic architecture after its grand Italianate period. It was the precursor of the mock-Tudor mansions and brick 'cottages' of suburbia.

Life in Red House turned out to be very like life in Red Lion Square. There was again a constant stream of visitors, and yet more

The garden front (*above*) and the entrance hall of Red House (*left*), the medieval home which Philip Webb designed for Morris in 1859. Rossetti described it as 'more a poem than a house . . . but an admirable place to live in too'. The house was striking in its simplicity, both inside and out. Webb designed most of the furniture, including the massive settle-cupboard in the entrance hall which was painted with scenes from the *Nibelungenlied*.

Tiles designed by Morris for the garden porch, Red House, incorporating his motto, *Si Je Puis.*

Morris's original design for 'Flamma Troiae', an embroidered panel for Red House.

practical jokes. Friends played on Morris's fear of getting fat and put a tuck in his waistcoat at night. 'You fellows have been at it again,' he complained. He himself was engrossed in the task of decorating the house, and was constantly experimenting with new techniques. He made tiles for the porch, stained-glass for the windows and embroidery for the hangings. Everyone who came to stay at Red House was given a paint-brush and told to help with the decoration. Morris pricked out holes in the ceiling to guide the brushes of the unskilled. Burne-Jones covered the walls of the drawing-room with scenes from the medieval romance of Sire Degrevaunt while Rossetti painted 'the Salutation of Beatrice' on the doors of the great settle from Red Lion Square. This had been given a parapet to act as both a minstrels' gallery and an access route to the loft, a touching combination of the romantic and the practical. Meanwhile Jane Morris and Elizabeth Siddal busied themselves with embroidering bed-hangings.

It was as a direct result of these efforts to decorate Red House that Morris conceived the idea of going into business to design and make furniture and works of art. The Devon mining shares on which he depended for his livelihood were going steadily down in value, and it was clear that he would have to find another source of income. 'The idea came to him,' Burne-Jones later recalled, 'of beginning a manufactory of all things necessary for the decoration of a house. Webb had already designed some beautiful table glass, made by Powell of Whitefriars, metal candlesticks, and tables for Red House, and I had already designed several windows for churches, so the idea grew of putting our experience together for the service of the public.'

The decision to set up a commercial firm specializing in the decorative arts was taken very casually, and was, characteristically, inspired by the example of the medieval craft guilds. Rossetti recalled:

One evening a lot of us were together, and we got talking about the way in which artists did all kinds of things in olden times, designed every kind of decoration and most kinds of furniture, and someone suggested – as a joke more than anything else – that we should each put down £5 and form a company. Fivers were blossoms of a rare growth among us in those days, and I won't swear that the table bristled with fivers. Anyhow the firm was formed, but of course there was no deed or anything of that kind. In fact, it was a mere playing at business and Morris was elected manager, not because we ever dreamed he would turn out to be a man of business, but because he was the only one of us who had time and money to spare.

On 11 April 1861, Morris, Marshall, Faulkner & Company issued a prospectus advertising their services as 'Fine Art Workmen in Painting, Carving, Furniture and the Metals'. At the head of the prospectus were printed the names of the founder-members of the firm: Ford Madox Brown, Edward Burne-Jones, Charles Faulkner, P. P. Marshall, William Morris, D. G. Rossetti and Philip Webb. Each of them held a single share in the company. Two of the members were not primarily artists or designers: Marshall was a surveyor and sanitary engineer who was a friend of Brown, and Faulkner had given up a mathematics fellowship at Oxford to become the company's first book-keeper. He received an annual salary of £150, as did Morris for being manager. The prospectus informed potential customers that the firm would be producing mural decorations, carvings, stained-glass windows, metalwork, furniture and embroidery.

Morris & Company were anything but modest about their capabilities. The prospectus began:

The growth of Decorative Art in this country, owing to the efforts of English Architects, has now reached a point at which it seems desirable that Artists of reputation should devote their time to it. Although no doubt particular instances of success may be cited, still it must be generally felt that attempts of this kind hitherto have been crude and fragmentary. Up to this time, the want of that artistic supervision, which can alone bring about harmony between the various parts of a successful work, has been increased by the necessarily excessive outlay, consequent on taking one individual artist from his pictorial labours. The Artists whose names appear above hope by association to do away with this difficulty.

Glassware designed by Philip Webb in 1859, and later sold by Morris, Marshall, Faulkner & Co.

There was, in fact, nothing new about the idea of reviving and encouraging the useful and decorative arts in the mid-nineteenth century. Prince Albert had tried hard to arouse interest in the establishment of an English Academy of Practical Arts in the 1840s, and Henry Cole, the organizer of the Great Exhibition of 1851, had

'The Sermon on the Mount', a design by Rossetti for stained glass. Altogether, Morris & Co. executed stained-glass windows for over four hundred buildings in Britain and abroad.

Morris wearing the round hat and blouse in which he always worked.

founded the South Kensington Museum (now the Victoria and Albert) to exhibit 'examples of fine workmanship in the applied arts of all times and people'. In 1847 Cole had even set up a company, Summerly's Art Manufactures, to design decorative objects and furniture. Like nearly all other enterprises of the time, it relied on techniques of mass-production. It was against this factory-production of objects for the home, which cluttered Victorian drawing-rooms with tasteless knick-knacks, that Morris and his associates revolted.

What was new about Morris & Co. was their insistence that artists should involve themselves in the actual processes of production, and not leave this to factory-labourers. They wanted to revive the medieval ideal of the artist craftsman who designed and executed his own work, with the result that, from original conception to finished product, it never passed out of his hands. In fact, of course, this ideal was not always realized. The firm used outside craftsmen for making furniture and for printing the wallpapers and textiles designed by its members. It even used machines for some printing and weaving work, when it was satisfied that this did not produce inferior results. But the ideal of medieval craftsmanship remained an important guiding principle, particularly for Morris himself, who insisted that he master the techniques of producing a particular art-form before he started designing for it.

The firm set up business in rented premises a few doors away from Morris's and Burne-Jones's old rooms in Red Lion Square. The showroom and office were on the first floor and the workshops on the third. A small kiln was built in the basement for firing glass and tiles. As the volume of work grew, several local workmen were taken on as employees, including a group of lads from a Boys' Home in the Euston Road. Morris and Faulkner were the only members of the firm who attended regularly at its offices. Marshall, Burne-Jones, Rossetti, Webb and Brown put in fairly frequent appearances to draw up designs for stained-glass windows. Female relatives of the firm's members were much in evidence at Red Lion Square. Faulkner's two sisters, Kate and Lucy, helped to paint pottery and tiles, many of which were designed by the famous potter William de Morgan, who never actually joined the firm although he worked closely with it. Jane Morris and her sister Elizabeth Burden took charge of the embroidery, helped by Burne-Jones's wife, Georgiana, who also assisted in painting tiles.

The financial affairs of the firm were predictably chaotic. None of the members was interested in that side of its activities, and least of all the manager. Prospective customers would be greeted by Morris in his round hat and blue workman's blouse, and would be left in no doubt that he was far more interested in getting on with the work in hand than in discussing new commissions. The weekly meetings of the

company concentrated more on debating the relative merits of thirteenth- and fourteenth-century art than on dealing with urgent business matters. There was no proper system of costing jobs or spreading the work out evenly among the members. The firm had not been established on a proper financial footing and it was permanently under-capitalized. In January 1862 a further call of £19 from each of the shareholders brought its paid-up capital to £140, but most of its working capital had to come from Morris's own dwindling revenue from the mining shares.

Luckily, it did not require any business acumen to sell in mid-Victorian Britain the kind of products that Morris & Co. were making. The cult of medievalism and the Anglo-Catholic movement in the Church of England created a ready market for their work. Morris asked his old Oxford tutor for a list of High Church clergymen to whom it might be useful to send a prospectus; and the firm's good showing at the International Exhibition at South Kensington in 1862 gave it its first commissions. Among its exhibits in the Medieval Court were seven stained-glass panels by Rossetti – *The Parable of the Vineyard*. Other exhibitors complained that these resembled medieval glass so closely that they must, in fact, be old glass touched-up. They attracted the attention of the High Church architect G. F. Bodley,

The original cartoon by Morris for 'St Paul Preaching at Athens' (*above*) and the stained-glass window (*above right*) for which it was designed, in Bodley's new church at Selsley, Gloucestershire (1862). It was one of a hundred and fifty church windows designed by Morris before he decided it was wrong to reproduce medieval art in modern buildings.

who promptly commissioned the firm to design and make windows for his new churches at Selsley in Gloucestershire, in Brighton and Scarborough, and for Jesus College Chapel and All Saints' Church in Cambridge.

Stained-glass windows were by far the most numerous and important of the firm's products in its early years. Morris himself designed over one hundred and fifty windows, as well as drawing the backgrounds for many more. Rossetti, Madox Brown and Webb were between them equally productive, and Burne-Jones, who was the most talented and popular designer of stained glass in the firm, did many more. The cartoons for windows came to Morris, who controlled the overall colour scheme, set the leading lines, chose the glass and supervised the painting and making of the windows. In conjunction with George Campfield, the foreman at the Red Lion Square works, who was an experienced glass-painter, Morris developed a yellow stain which enabled him to produce a range of tints and tones from pale yellow to red bronze, and which gave an equivalent effect on glass to embroidered and damask designs on cloth. In the opinion of Professor A. C. Sewter, the author of the standard work on the subject, the best windows produced by Morris & Co. attained a higher level of quality than had been seen in England since the sixteenth century. Where earlier Victorians merely made poor imitations of medieval glass, Morris was innovatory and original.

Orders for furniture provided the firm with its second most important source of work in its early years. A wall-cabinet designed by Webb with doors painted by Morris to depict the legend of St George, and a large cabinet designed by J. P. Seddon and covered by Rossetti, Burne-Jones, Madox Brown and Morris with imaginary incidents in the honeymoon of King René of Anjou, had both attracted considerable attention at the firm's stand at the 1862 International Exhibition. Despite his early efforts at Red Lion Square, Morris never designed any furniture for the company. Much of the firm's early furniture was designed by Philip Webb and was, in the words of the catalogue, 'of solid construction and joiner-made'. It was often painted by Morris, Burne-Jones and Rossetti. To modern eyes Webb's tables and dressers may appear somewhat heavy, but they were certainly simpler and more solid than the furniture found in most mid-Victorian English drawing-rooms.

Although he himself did not design furniture, Morris regarded it as perhaps the most significant of the firm's products. It was particularly important in his estimation because it was something that was found in every home and combined the qualities of beauty and utility. For Morris, these two ideals could best be achieved by absolute simplicity

'King Arthur and Sir Lancelot', a cartoon with figure of Arthur by Morris and Lancelot by Ford Madox Brown for a series of windows illustrating 'The Story of Tristram' (1862).

Panel painted by Morris showing the legend of St George on the front of a wall-cabinet designed by Webb in 1861 and exhibited at the 1862 International Exhibition.

Above, the simplicity and elegance of the Panelled Room in Morris's house at Kelmscott contrasts with the clutter (*right*) of a typical mid-Victorian drawing room (1867). The round table (*left*) in the Panelled Room is by Philip Webb and there is a 'Rossetti' style rush-seated armchair by the fireplace. This interior may well have promoted the fashion for white sitting-rooms, which is still followed.

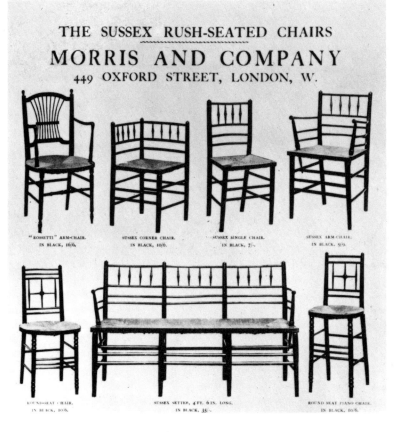

THE SUSSEX RUSH-SEATED CHAIRS
MORRIS AND COMPANY
449 OXFORD STREET, LONDON, W.

"ROSSETTI" ARM-CHAIR. IN BLACK, 16/6.
SUSSEX CORNER CHAIR. IN BLACK, 10/6.
SUSSEX SINGLE CHAIR. IN BLACK, 7/-.
SUSSEX ARM-CHAIR. IN BLACK, 9/9.
ROUND-SEAT CHAIR. IN BLACK, 10/6.
SUSSEX SETTEE, 4 FT. 6 IN. LONG. IN BLACK, 35/-.
ROUND SEAT PIANO CHAIR. IN BLACK, 10/6.

The Sussex rush-seated chairs, which became one of the most popular items made by Morris & Co., were copied from an old chair discovered by George Warrington Taylor, the firm's business manager, on a visit to Sussex in the late 1860s.

of design. 'Our furniture', he wrote, 'should be good citizens' furniture, solid and well made in workmanship, and in design should have nothing about it that is not easily defensible, no monstrosities or extravagances, not even of beauty, lest we weary of it.' This led him to reject utterly the prevailing Empire and Rococo styles of domestic furniture, which were heavily embellished with brass, marble and leather, and also extremely unpractical and uncomfortable. Instead, he went back to traditional early English styles, most notably in the Sussex rush-seated chairs and the adjustable-back chair that were the firm's most popular products. What attracted Morris to these was not their style so much as their construction. For him craftsmanship was more important than aesthetics.

Morris & Co. also produced a wide range of smaller decorative objects in their early years. In the 1862 Exhibition they showed candlesticks and jewellery designed by Webb, tiles painted by Rossetti and various pieces of embroidery. Webb continued to design a large number of household objects for the firm, including distinctive lampstands and table glass. Tiles were always a popular product.

The 'Morris' adjustable-back armchair, developed by Webb from a Sussex type, c. 1866.

Some of the firm's products: earthenware tiles of scenes from *The Sleeping Beauty* designed by Burne-Jones, with swan tiles by Webb (*above*); tiles by de Morgan, Burne-Jones and Webb (*above right*). An embroidered panel (*below*) of *c.* 1877 and an embroidered hanging, St Catherine (*below right*), were both designed by Morris.

Initially they were imported in plain earthenware from Holland and then handpainted by members of the firm and fired in the kiln at Red Lion Square. But later on the firm manufactured its own tiles, most of which were designed by Morris and William de Morgan. Morris also designed most of the firm's embroideries. These were sold to customers either ready-made, or as patterns together with hand-dyed silk or wool.

Morris designed the first of his forty-one wallpapers, the 'Trellis', in 1862. Wallpaper-design probably appealed to him more than any other decorative art and, of all the firm's activities, it was certainly the one best suited to his own particular talents. Ever since his boyhood visit to the room hung with tapestries at Chingford Hatch, he had regarded wall-coverings as an especially beautiful and exciting form of decoration. As he put it in a lecture on *The Lesser Arts of Life*, 'To turn our chamber walls into the green woods of the leafy month of June, populous of bird and beast; or a summer garden with man and maid playing round a fountain, or a solemn procession of the mythical warriors and heroes of old; that surely was worth the trouble of doing.' In fact there were to be no maidens or warriors in any of Morris's wallpapers. He built his designs entirely around the motifs of flower, leaf and bird which he had loved as a boy. This allowed him to display his mastery of these shapes without requiring him to draw any human figures. Although his wallpapers were full of pattern and movement they were always representational and never abstract. 'As a Western

Below left, The 'Trellis', Morris's first wallpaper, designed in 1862. The pattern probably derives from the Rose Trellis at Red House. *Above* and *below*, 'Wild Tulip', original design and finished wallpaper for one of Morris's last wallpapers (1884). By then, his designs had become less stylized and more flowing.

'Fruit' wallpaper, 1864. Morris wrote of wallpaper design, 'the aim should be to combine clearness of form and firmness of structure with the mystery which comes from abundance and richness of detail.'

man and a picture lover,' he once commented, 'I must still insist on plenty of meaning to your patterns; I must have unmistakable suggestions of gardens and fields, and strange trees, boughs and tendrils.'

Most of Morris's wallpapers were hand-printed for the firm by Messrs Jeffrey & Company of Islington. His designs were cut on to pear-wood blocks which were then inked and used for printing the papers. It was a lengthy and laborious process compared with machine-printing, but it allowed each colour to be printed separately. Morris closely supervised the work. The blocks were cut by workmen, but the cutter's tracings were always submitted to him for retouching before they were rubbed off the wood. Once the blocks were cut, the success of the printing depended entirely on the care and fidelity of the colour-mixers. Morris kept a careful eye on their pots of distemper to make sure that they achieved exactly the right result.

Many of Morris's wallpapers were commissioned for particular houses by individual owners and did not, therefore, need to be produced in large quantities. Morris himself was responsible for designing and supervising the printing of the majority of the wallpapers sold by the firm, although Kate Faulkner and J. H. Dearle, who joined Morris & Co. in 1878, also designed papers and helped in their production.

Before long the firm was undertaking complete schemes of interior decoration, involving furniture, wallpaper, and painted ceilings and friezes, for both public and private clients. In 1866 it received two important commissions, the decoration of the Green Dining Room at the South Kensington Museum and the Armoury and Tapestry Rooms at St James's Palace. They show how quickly Morris & Co.'s fame had spread, even to the Establishment, but they came too late to prevent a financial crisis. In November 1865 lack of money, and the difficulty of making the long daily journey to work from the country, had forced Morris and Jane, and their two young daughters May and Jenny, to leave Red House and move in above new premises which the firm had taken in Queen Square, Bloomsbury. The previous year Faulkner had resigned in desperation after trying vainly to bring some order into the firm's financial affairs. He was replaced as book-keeper by George Warrington Taylor, who had been at Eton with Swinburne, served in the army and then became a check-taker at a London opera-house where he was able to indulge his love of music. Taylor laboured hard until his early death in 1870 to keep the firm from going bankrupt. It was an uphill struggle, little helped by Morris's habit of continually signing small cheques for himself, drawn on the company's meagre funds. Taylor complained to Morris that he took on far more jobs than the firm could manage and then left them half-done, and he begged him to give up entertaining and reduce his wine consumption to two and a half bottles a day. Morris responded

by temporarily lessening his own involvement in the work of the firm and withdrawing into a more private world. He took to writing poetry again. In 1867 he published *The Life and Death of Jason*, a long epic based on the classical story of the quest for the Golden Fleece. This received much more favourable reviews from the critics than *The Defence of Guenevere*. Even greater acclaim was in store. In 1868 he brought out the first volume of *The Earthly Paradise*, which was to be his most popular poetic work.

The Earthly Paradise is a collection of twenty-four stories taken from medieval, classical, Eastern and Norse legends, told by a group of wanderers who have fled from a plagued city to an Atlantic island where Greek and North European cultures meet. The theme is essentially one of escape. The stories present a picture of a secure,

The Green Dining Room designed by Philip Webb for the South Kensington Museum (now the Victoria and Albert). The walls, frieze and ceiling are by Webb, the grand piano has gesso work by Kate Faulkner, the embroidered screen by William and Jane Morris has illustrations from Chaucer's *Legende of Good Women*, and the St George Cabinet is under the window at the back. The room was Morris & Co.'s first important commission.

unchanging past in contrast to the discord and tumult of the present. In the Prologue the reader is invited to:

> *Forget six counties overhung with smoke,*
> *Forget the snorting steam and piston stroke,*
> *Forget the spreading of the hideous town;*
> *Think rather of the pack-horse on the down,*
> *And dream of London small, and white, and clean,*
> *The clear Thames bordered by its gardens green.*

The atmosphere of *The Earthly Paradise* is dream-like. Lacking any strong rhythmic beat, the verses amble on in a leisurely and archaic style. It is almost too effortless in construction, perhaps because of the circumstance of its composition. Morris wrote much of the poem on train journeys between London and Oxford, where he and Jane took lodgings with the Faulkners and Burne-Jones in the summer of 1857. The rest of it was thought up while he was designing for the firm. He would work out about twenty lines in his head and then rush to his desk to commit them to paper. He completed the poem at considerable speed, often writing seven hundred lines a day.

Because of its easy style and its escapist theme *The Earthly Paradise* became a favourite poem with the Victorians. Reviewers were generally enthusiastic and stressed its suitability for family reading. *The Saturday Review* described it as ideal 'for conveying to our wives and daughters a refined, although not diluted version of those wonderful creations of Greek fancy which the rougher sex alone is permitted to imbibe at first hand'. *The Earthly Paradise* firmly confirmed Morris as a leading poet in the eyes of his contemporaries. It also established their view of him as a harmless romantic and medievalist, detached from

A caricature by Burne-Jones of Morris cutting a wood block for a projected illustrated edition of *The Earthly Paradise*, 1865, abandoned because of printing difficulties.

THE

EARTHLY PARADISE

A POEM.

BY

WILLIAM MORRIS,

AUTHOR OF THE LIFE AND DEATH OF JASON.

London : F. S. ELLIS, 33 *King Street, Covent Garden.*
MDCCCLXVIII.

contemporary concerns. He had, after all, described himself in these terms in the Apology at the start of the work:

> *Dreamer of dreams, born out of my due time,*
> *Why should I strive to set the crooked straight?*
> *Let it suffice me that my murmuring rhyme*
> *Beats with light wing against the ivory gate,*
> *Telling a tale not too importune*
> *To those who in the sleepy region stay,*
> *Lulled by the singer of an empty day.*

There was, however, another, darker side to *The Earthly Paradise* than the idle escapism and romantic medievalism which captivated the Victorians. The work is pervaded by a sense of despair, and

Above left, Title page of the 1868 edition of *The Earthly Paradise*, with the *Three Musicians*, an engraving by Morris.

Pull from one of the wood blocks engraved by Morris from drawings by Burne-Jones for the projected 1865 edition of *The Earthly Paradise*.

41

Rossetti, photographed by Lewis Carroll in 1863, shortly before he began his close relationship with Jane Morris. He is already showing signs of the illness and corpulence which afflicted him in later life.

Opposite, Jane Morris, posed by Rossetti and photographed in the garden of his house in Cheyne Walk in 1865. The photograph recalls Henry James' description of her as 'a tall lean woman, with a mass of crisp black hair heaped into great wavy projections on each side of her temples, a thin pale face, a pair of strange, sad, deep, dark Swinburnian eyes, with great thick black oblique brows, joined in the middle and tucking themselves away under her hair, and a long neck, without any collar'.

specifically by the theme of lost love, as in this passage from the poem 'September.'

> Look long, O longing eyes, and look in vain!
> Strain idly, aching heart, and yet be wise
> And hope no more for things to come again
> That thou beholdest once with careless eyes!
> Like a new wakened man thou art, who tries
> To dream again the dream that made him glad
> When in his arms his loving love he had.

Morris had become increasingly conscious that in their nine years of marriage his relationship with Jane had never progressed from the idealized illusion of romantic love to a level of real tenderness and understanding. As she became more estranged from Morris, Jane was drawn closer to Rossetti. During the late 1860s the two of them were often seen together at studio parties which Morris did not attend. In 1870 Edmund Gosse described them at a gathering at Madox Brown's house in Fitzroy Square, Jane sitting on the model's throne like a queen in a long ivory velvet dress and Rossetti, 'too stout for elegance', perched on a hassock at her feet. A cousin of William de Morgan recalled seeing them at another party sitting together in a corner with Rossetti feeding Jane strawberries, and both of them oblivious to everyone else in the room.

There is no doubt that Rossetti was deeply in love with Jane. She responded to his passion for her despite the fact that addiction to laudanum and frequent bouts of insomnia were turning him into a physical and psychological wreck. He offered her the tenderness and affection that her husband never showed. Jane was now almost permanently unwell herself. In the summer of 1869 Morris took her to the spa at Bad-Ems in Hesse-Nassau in an effort to cure her, although he made no secret of the fact that he regarded the trip as a tedious interruption of his work. Rossetti wrote to Jane in terms which make clear his love for her:

I can never tell you how much I am with you at all times. Absence from your sight is what I have long been used to: and no absence can ever make me so far from you again as your presence did for years. For this long inconceivable change, you know now what my thanks must be. But I have no right to talk to you in a way that may make you sad on my account, when in reality the balance of joy and sorrow is now so much more in my favour than it has been or could have hoped to become, for years past.

Caricature sent by Rossetti to Jane when Morris, in the middle of writing *The Earthly Paradise*, had taken her for a cure to the spa at Bad-Ems in July 1869, 'to prepare you for the worst – whichever that may be, the seven tumblers [of spa water] or the seven volumes [of the book]'.

Rossetti expressed his feelings for Jane in a series of portraits which gave her a strange, quasi-mystical sexuality, and in increasingly overt love poems. His published collection of poems which appeared in 1870 contained many verses inspired by Jane as well as earlier ones to

Kelmscott Manor, Oxfordshire.
Above, the east front, showing the
sixteenth-century house with the
addition of about 1670 on the right,
and *right*, Morris's bedroom. The bed
hangings were designed by May
Morris and took more than forty
weeks to embroider, much of the
work being done by Lucy Yeats,
sister of the poet W.B. Yeats.

Rossetti's *La Pia de' Tolomei*, 1880. This painting, for which Jane Morris was the model, depicts the confinement of Pia de' Tolomei by her husband in a fortress of the Maremma, as related in the Fifth Canto of Dante's *Purgatorio*. For both artist and sitter, the parallel with their own situation must have been striking.

Elizabeth Siddal. Ironically, Morris had to review the poems for *The Academy*. He was unqualified in his praise of the poems and showed no sign of bitterness at the publication by another of intimate verses addressed to his own wife.

To the outside world, Morris still appeared to be a happy family man. In May 1871 he wrote to Faulkner, 'I have been looking around for a house for the wife and kids, and whither do you guess my eye is turned now? Kelmscott, a little village above Radcott Bridge – a heaven on earth, an old stone Elizabethan house like Water Eaton, and such a garden! close down by the river, a boathouse and all things handy.' Morris and Rossetti took a joint tenancy of Kelmscott Manor, which stands on the north bank of the Thames near Lechlade on the borders of Gloucestershire and Oxfordshire, and shared the rent of £60 a year. Rossetti promptly took up residence at Kelmscott with Jane, and for the next three years they spent long periods living together there. Morris kept away from Kelmscott when Rossetti and Jane were both there and stayed at Horrington House, a small house in Chiswick which he bought at the end of 1872. He accepted their relationship with remarkable forbearance, showing no animosity to the wife who had proved unfaithful or the friend who had cuckolded him, beyond complaining once to another friend in 1872 that 'Rossetti has set himself down at Kelmscott as if he never meant to go away; and not only does that keep me from the harbour of my refuge (because it is really a farce our meeting when we can help it) but also he has all sorts of ways so unsympathetic with the sweet simple old place, that I feel his presence there as a kind of slur on it.'

Morris saw so little of his new country-house, indeed, that in 1874 he seriously considered giving up his share of the tenancy. But that summer was to be Rossetti's last in Kelmscott. His peculiar behaviour and increasingly depressed state had made him the subject of much gossip in the village, and when he hysterically attacked a group of local fishermen whom he thought had insulted him, it was felt best that he should leave the place for good. His close relationship with Jane continued until his death in 1882, although it was pursued mostly through letters and they never lived together again. Morris and Jane became further estranged as a result of the affair with Rossetti, although they continued to live an outwardly normal family life together and to to go on Continental holidays with the children.

Morris's acceptance of Rossetti's affair with Jane was in marked contrast to the behaviour expected of the wronged husband in Victorian times. He believed that marriage was not a property-contract to be enforced at all costs, and that husband and wife should always remain free agents. When he became a socialist he was to argue for the marriage contract to be 'voluntary and unenforced by the community . . . nor would a truly enlightened public opinion, freed from mere theological views as to chastity, insist on its permanently binding nature in the face of any discomfort or suffering that might come of it'. But for all his advanced views on the subject, there was no doubt that the failure of his own marriage was a crippling blow to him. A poem, 'Love Is Enough', written in the autumn of 1871, reveals the despair and sense of emptiness which were threatening to overwhelm him:

Love is enough: draw near and behold me
Ye who pass by the way to your rest and your laughter,
And are full of the hope of the dawn coming after;
For the strong of the world have bought me and sold me
And my house is all wasted from threshold to rafter,
Pass by me, and hearken, and think of me not!

Morris found some escape from the unhappiness of his personal life in the company of his oldest friends. In November 1868 Edward and Georgiana Burne-Jones moved their home to The Grange in Fulham. Morris took to visiting them every Sunday for breakfast and often stayed for the rest of the day. These regular visits continued until the end of his life. He became particularly close to 'Georgie', who gave him the warmth and understanding which Jane never showed, and who herself had to come to terms with her husband's romantic escapades.

Opposite, Morris and Burne-Jones in the garden of The Grange, Fulham, 1874.

Georgiana Burne-Jones painted by
Sir Edward Poynter, 1870. Morris
found increasing consolation in her
company.

Jane Morris adopting the soulful pose
so beloved by the Pre-Raphaelites,
photographed in Rossetti's home in
Cheyne Walk.

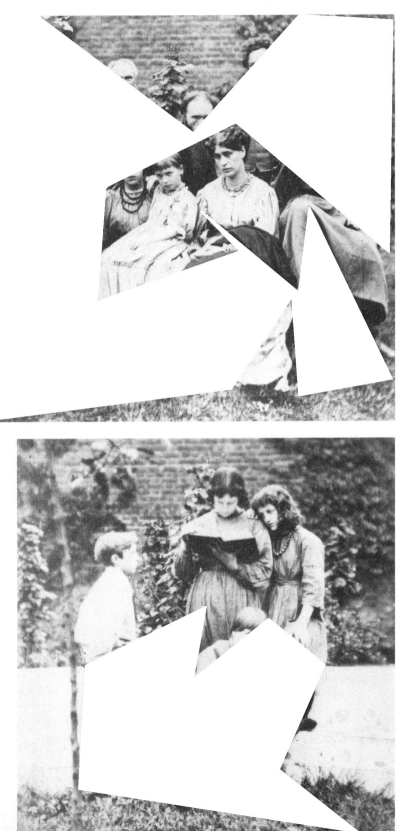

The Morris and Burne-Jones families,
photographed by Hollyer, 1874.
From left to right: Georgiana Burne-
Jones, Philip Burne-Jones, Burne-
Jones's father, Jenny Morris, Margaret
Burne-Jones, Edward Burne-Jones,
Jane Morris, William Morris and
May Morris.

The Morris and Burne-Jones children
in the garden of The Grange,
Fulham.

Caricature by Burne-Jones of himself
and Morris having Sunday lunch at
The Grange, with Philip Burne-
Jones looking on, c. 1875–8.

HAVE I been hearkening
To some dread new-comer?
What chain is it bindeth,
What curse is anigh,
That the World is a-darkening
Amidmost the summer,
That the soft sunset blindeth
And Death standeth by?

Doth it wane, is it going,
Is it gone by for ever,
The life that seemed round me,
The longing I sought?
Has it turned to undoing
That constant endeavour
To bind love that bound me,
To hold all it brought?

I beheld till beholding
Grew pain thrice told over;
I hearkened till hearing
Grew woe beyond speech;
I dreamed of enfolding
Arms blessing the lover

With Georgiana as his once inspiration, Morris turned again to the delicate art of manuscript illumination which he had first practised as a pupil in Street's office. In 1870, with the help of Burne-Jones and others, he produced *A Book of Verse*, and two years later he began work on an edition of *The Rubaiyat of Omar Khayyam*. Both works were presented to Georgiana. In 1875 he designed an edition of Horace's *Odes*, and worked with Burne-Jones on an illuminated manuscript of Virgil's *Aeneid* which he translated at the same time.

It was his immersion in the literature and culture of Iceland which really dispelled Morris's unhappiness in the early 1870s and set his life on a new course. He had long been aware of the Norse sagas and had, indeed, included romanticized versions of them in his poetry. But he had not seen the North as having a separate cultural identity of its own, essentially different from the romance and chivalry which prevailed in the rest of medieval Europe. Now, in exploring the rugged culture and the frozen wastes of Iceland, he found not just an echo of his own sense of desolation, but a source of courage and hope which was to transform

Page from Horace's *Odes*, transcribed and decorated by Morris in 1875.

Opposite, 'Lonely Love and Loveless Death', a poem from *A Book of Verse*, written and decorated by Morris in 1870. He presented it to Georgiana Burne-Jones.

him from 'the idle singer of an empty day' into a passionate political activist and reformer. The experience of Iceland finally ended Morris's medieval escapism, and inspired him to go out and do things in the modern world. 'In Norse literature', he wrote, 'I found a good corrective to the maundering side of medievalism.'

Morris's interest in Iceland dated from the autumn of 1868 when Warrington Taylor had introduced him to Eirikr Magnusson, an Icelandic scholar who had come to England in 1862 to supervise publication of a Norse New Testament and start work on a Norse dictionary. Magnusson was curiously like Morris in both physique and temperament. He paced up and down his room singing Norse folk songs in a loud voice. Not surprisingly, Morris took strongly to him. 'Altogether,' he wrote, 'what with his personal appearance, his peculiarly frank manner, his insatiable curiosity, exuberant hilarity and transparent serious mindedness, I felt I had never come across a more attractive personality.' Morris proposed that Magnusson should teach him Icelandic. He was an eager pupil, often going to Magnusson three times a week for three hour lessons, although his impatience to get to the literature led him largely to ignore grammar. He ordered Magnusson: 'You be my grammar as we go along.' The two men worked systematically through the sagas, with Magnusson producing a first literal translation and Morris rewriting it for publication. Their first translation, *The Saga of Gunnlaug Worm Tongue*, appeared in the *Fortnightly Review* of January 1869. The next, *The Grettis Saga*, was published later that year and *The Volsung Saga* appeared in 1870. On the whole, Morris stuck faithfully to the original themes of the sagas and wrote in close imitation of Norse vocabulary and syntax. But he was unable to avoid reflecting his own troubles in his translations. The theme of *The Volsung Saga*, he wrote in the Prologue, was:

> *Of utter love defeated utterly,*
> *Of Grief too strong to give Love time to die.*

But the magic of the sagas was weaving its spell around him. He was determined to go to the land that had inspired them. So, early in July 1871, as Rossetti and Jane were settling into Kelmscott for the summer, Morris set off for Iceland with Faulkner, Magnusson and W. H. Evans, an army officer.

Morris's two journeys to Iceland, in 1871 and 1873, were as important in changing the future course of his life as his two visits to France as an undergraduate. The eerie landscape of frozen wastes broken only by volcanoes and waterfalls affected him powerfully. 'It was like nothing I had ever seen,' he wrote of the Faroe Islands on the voyage out, 'but strangely like my old imaginations of places for sea wanderers to come to . . . a most beautiful and poetical place it looked to me, but more remote and melancholy than I can say, in spite of the

Binding for the 1870 edition of *The Story of the Volsungs and Niblungs*, translated from the Icelandic by Morris and Magnusson. The green cloth binding with stamped gold pattern was designed by Morris and Philip Webb.

flowers and grass and bright sun: it looked as though you might live for a hundred years before you would ever see ship sailing into the bay there; as if the old life of the saga-time had gone, and the modern life had never reached the place.' He was struck by this timelessness and remoteness, and by the stark conditions of life imposed on the inhabitants. 'It is an awful place,' he wrote in his journal after his visit to Iceland, 'set aside the hope that the unseen sea gives you here and the strange threatening change of the spiky mountains beyond the firth, and the rest seems emptiness and nothing else: a piece of turf under your feet, and the sky overhead, that's all: whatever solace your life is to have must come out of yourself or these old stories, not over hopeful themselves.'

What impressed Morris above all was the bravery and sturdiness of the Icelanders in the face of these desolate conditions. 'The delightful

A nineteenth-century photograph of
a scene near Reykjavik in Iceland.
Morris described the country as 'a
great mass of dark grey mountains
worked into pyramids and shelves,
looking as if they had been built and
half-ruined'. He was much affected
by the starkness and ruggedness of
the Icelandic landscape, and by the
hardiness of the inhabitants.

Caricature by Burne-Jones of Morris
eating fish in Iceland. Rossetti wrote,
'Morris has come back from Iceland
more enslaved with passion for ice
and snow and raw fish than ever.'

freshness and independence of thought in them,' he later wrote, 'the air of freedom which breathes through them, their worship of courage (the great virtue of the human race) took my heart by storm.' The hardy Norseman replaced the medieval craftsman as the main model for Morris's own behaviour. In the Icelanders' closely-knit tribal society he discovered a truth which was to be fundamental to his future thinking: 'I learned that the most grinding poverty is a trifling evil compared with the inequality of classes.' Iceland had given Morris new hope, new ideals and new convictions. It had impressed on him above all the potentiality of man to rise above his surroundings and to achieve great things through his own effort. He wrote after his second trip to Iceland of 'the glorious simplicity of the terrible and tragic, but beautiful land, with its well remembered stories of brave men', and concluded, 'I feel as if a definite space of my life had passed away, now that I have seen Iceland for the last time.'

The immediate legacy of Morris's discovery of Iceland was his epic poem, *Sigurd the Volsung*, published in 1876. It is generally agreed to be his greatest poetic achievement, although it was not seen as such by some of his friends. Swinburne, for instance, had no time for 'all that dashed and blank Volsungery which will end by eating up the splendid genius it has already overgrown and encrusted with Icelandic moss'. Morris himself considered *Sigurd the Volsung* to be the central work of his life. In its vast scale and subject-matter it is reminiscent of Wagner's Ring cycle of operas. Morris portrays the death of the Gods as the overthrow of competition and war, and sees it as heralding the dawning of a new era of peace and happiness. *Sigurd the Volsung* is a work of hope, looking forward to:

> *The last of the days of the battle, when the host of the Gods is arrayed*
> *And there is an end forever to all who were once afraid*

and to the time

> *When the new light yet undreamed of shall shine o'er earth and sea.*

The long-term effect of Morris's Icelandic experience was to make him much more concerned with contemporary problems and involved in public affairs in the last twenty-five years of his life.

The first manifestation of this new-found interest in political questions was his participation in the national agitation over the Bulgarian atrocities in 1876. The brutal suppression by the Turks of a revolt by their Bulgarian subjects, involving the massacre of twelve thousand men, women and children, aroused the anger of many sensitive Victorian consciences. They were even more incensed when the Prime Minister, Disraeli, far from censuring the Turks, threatened to take Britain to war against Russia in their support. The ensuing campaign against the war, which was fired by Gladstone's publication

Algernon Charles Swinburne from his friend William Morris

THE STORY
OF
SIGURD THE VOLSUNG
AND THE
FALL OF THE NIBLUNGS.

A copy of *Sigurd the Volsung* sent by Morris to Swinburne. Like most of Morris's friends, however, Swinburne was not much impressed by the book and could not understand its author's passion for all things Icelandic.

A *Punch* cartoon of August 1876 satirizing Disraeli's indifference to the Turks' massacre of their Bulgarian subjects. The caption reads, 'Bulgarian atrocities. I can't find them in the official reports.'

of his famous pamphlet, *The Bulgarian Atrocities and the Question of the East,* and which was organized by the Eastern Question Association, attracted the support of many Victorian writers and artists, including Tennyson, Trollope, Darwin, Carlyle, Ruskin and Burne-Jones.

Morris made his first public pronouncement on the Eastern Question, and indeed on any political matter, in a letter to the *Daily News* in October 1876. Just over a month later he was elected treasurer of the Eastern Question Association. Throughout 1877 he was active in campaigning against Disraeli's sabre-rattling, and when war between Russia and Turkey broke out in April, he brought out a pamphlet, *Unjust War: To The Working Men of England,* which warned against British involvement. In it, he pointed out that those who wanted war were 'greedy gamblers on the Stock Exchange, idle officers of the Army and Navy, worn-out mockers of the clubs, and desperate purveyors of exciting war news for the comfortable breakfast tables of those who have nothing to lose by war'. Although these were radical sentiments, they were no more so than those being voiced by Gladstone, who regularly denounced the upper ten thousand of the country for their support for war against the interests of the common people. Gladstone and Morris were both struck by the involvement of considerable numbers of ordinary working men in the campaign against Disraeli's Eastern policy. They differed, however, in the conclusions that they drew from this evidence of the political coming-of-age of the British working classes. Gladstone took it as a signal to embark on more crusades of a similar kind against injustices committed in foreign lands, in which he could whip up the moral indignation of the masses. Morris saw it rather as a sign that politics must increasingly be concerned with the domestic, social and economic issues which most affected working men. He later wrote that his own involvement in the Eastern Question campaign had come about principally because 'I thoroughly dreaded the outburst of chauvinism which swept over the country, and feared that once we were amusing ourselves with a European war no one in this country would listen to anything of social questions.'

Morris's first venture into politics and public life ended in disillusionment. It soon became clear to him that Gladstone and the Liberals were not really interested in maintaining their opposition to war with Russia, let alone in forwarding the social reforms which he was coming to see as essential. The Eastern Question Association was breaking up, and in January 1878 he wrote to Jane, 'As to my political career, I think it is at an end for the present.' In fact, he was soon back in active politics. In autumn 1879 he became Treasurer of the new National Liberal League which was formed out of the radical and working-class elements that had come together in the agitation over the Eastern Question. He worked hard with the League to rally the

Opposite, William Morris, aged 46, in 1880.

'Rupes Topseia', a caricature by Rossetti indicating his bitterness over Morris's reconstruction of the firm in 1875. Members of the original firm of Morris, Marshall, Faulkner & Co. sit in the background holding a scroll inscribed 'We are starving', while Jane Morris (top right), Marx and Engels look on as Morris descends towards Hell.

populace behind Gladstone's platform of 'Peace, Retrenchment and Reform' in the General Election of 1880. But the policies of the Liberal Government once it was in office, which included coercion in Ireland and the shelling of Alexandria in response to a rising of Egyptian nationalists, came as a great disappointment to Morris. At the end of 1881 he resigned from the National Liberal League and declared 'I do so hate everything vague in politics as well as in art.' He was well on the way to becoming a socialist.

First, however, Morris had to sort out the affairs of the firm which were in a considerable mess by the mid-1870s. Rossetti had become increasingly ill and was now suffering from a serious persecution complex. Brown, Marshall and Faulkner had ceased to take part in the work, which was now being entirely sustained by Morris, Burne-Jones and Webb. Morris proposed that the original firm be wound up and the non-productive partners retired. This happened in March 1875 when, after protracted wrangling, Brown, Marshall and Rossetti were each given £1,000 to compensate them for their loss of interest. This amount failed to satisfy Rossetti, who now became permanently estranged from Morris. The firm was re-established with Morris as sole manager, and Burne-Jones and Webb continuing to supply designs for stained glass and furniture.

The years following the reconstitution of the firm were Morris's most productive as a designer of wallpapers and textiles. Between 1876 and 1883 he designed eleven wallpapers and twenty-two chintzes. Textiles were now coming to replace stained glass and wallpaper as the firm's most popular products and Morris devoted himself to perfecting new techniques for colouring and producing them. He had been so unhappy with the colour of his first chintz, the 'Tulip and the Willow', designed in 1873 and printed by the leading calico-printer of the time, Thomas Clarkson of Preston, that it was not put on sale. Morris took his next chintz, the 'Tulip', to Thomas Wardle of Leek, Staffordshire, who was a well-known authority on dyeing and silk cultivation. Wardle, who was to print all of Morris's subsequent chintzes, allowed him to experiment with dyes himself until he got the right result.

The 'Tulip', the first chintz to be commercially produced by Morris & Co., 1875.

For Morris, dyeing was a classic example of a process where commercial considerations directly conflicted with artistic ones. The discovery of aniline dyes, produced from coal tar, in the Industrial Revolution had made dyeing much easier but produced cruder colours than those obtained from traditional vegetable dyes. Morris later wrote in his essay, *Of Dyeing as an Art*, 'Anyone wanting to produce dyed textiles of any artistic quality in them must entirely forego the modern and commercial methods in favour of those which are as old as Pliny, who speaks of them as being old in his time.' In his search for old, disused dyes, Morris went back to Pliny and to medieval herbals which he remembered looking at as a child. In October 1876 he went to Paris and searched thirteen shops for ancient herbals. He experimented continuously to find the best sources for different colours. Eventually he found that red was best obtained from the insect dye 'kermes' from Greece, yellow by boiling poplar and osier twigs together, brown from the roots of the walnut tree, and blue from indigo. Working in sabots and blouse, with his hands and elbows stained permanently blue, he spent several weeks experimenting in the indigo vats at Leek. The firm accumulated a large amount of stock as he painstakingly laboured to obtain exactly the right colours.

At the same time as he was learning how to dye, Morris was also exploring the art of weaving. At first he designed fabrics for machine production. In 1875 he produced his first design for a machine-woven

A wooden chair made by an apprentice for William Morris to use when weaving.

silk and wool fabric, the 'Anemone'. In the same year he produced the first of twenty-four designs for machine-made carpets which were woven by the Royal Wilton Carpet Works and the Heckmondwike Manufacturing Company in Yorkshire. In his work as an adviser to the Science and Art Department at the South Kensington Museum from 1876, he became interested in medieval hand-woven textiles from Spain and Sicily, and in Persian carpets. He also studied Flemish and Burgundian tapestries. The art of hand-weaving had died in England with the coming of the Industrial Revolution, and few tapestries had been produced since the closing of the Mortlake Royal Tapestry Works in the early eighteenth century. Morris taught himself the art of tapestry-weaving with the aid of an eighteenth-century French manual in the *Arts et Métiers* series. In 1877 he installed a Jacquard loom in the firm's workshop in a yard at the back of the Queen Square premises. He brought over a silk-weaver from Lyons to operate it, and employed an old Spitalfields weaver as his assistant. Most of Morris's brocades and furnishing silks were woven on this loom, although some damasks and the heavier woollen fabrics were woven by outside firms.

In October 1878 Morris and his family moved their London home from the cramped quarters at Horrington House to more spacious premises in Hammersmith while still retaining Kelmscott Manor as a

'Lily' Kidderminster carpet (*above left*), designed by Morris and probably machine-woven for Morris & Co. by an outside manufacturer, 1877, and (*above*) the 'Anemone', Morris's first design for a machine-woven fabric, 1875.

'Hammersmith' carpet, designed by Morris for Clouds in Wiltshire and woven on the looms set up in the old coach-house adjoining Kelmscott House, Hammersmith. Many of the Hammersmith carpets bore a trademark of a hammer and a wavy line symbolizing the Thames.

country retreat. Kelmscott House, as he named the new home, was a plain brick eighteenth-century building overlooking the Thames. In his bedroom Morris set up a tapestry loom on which he worked for as much as ten hours a day weaving the 'Cabbage and the Vine'. In the large coach-house which adjoined the property a carpet loom was installed, and a number of local women were taken on as weavers. It was here that the hand-knotted woollen pile 'Hammersmith' carpets and rugs were produced. In May 1880 Morris held an exhibition of them, and issued a circular in which he declared his aim as being 'to make England independent of the East for carpets which may claim to be considered as works of art'.

By 1880 weaving, dyeing and cotton printing had become Morris & Co.'s principal activities. It was impossible to carry out these processes in the cramped workshops at Queen Square, even with the additional space for weaving at the Hammersmith coach-house. In November 1881 the firm moved its workshops to Merton Abbey, near Morden in north Surrey. The site was ideal. It consisted of a group of sheds, which had previously housed a printing works, standing among willows and poplars on the bank of the River Wandle. The river water

Kelmscott House, Hammersmith, Morris's home for the last eighteen years of his life. Built in the 1780s, it is now the headquarters of the William Morris Society and houses visiting scholars.

The 'Cabbage and the Vine', the only tapestry designed and woven entirely by Morris himself. He produced it in 1879 on the tapestry loom which he set up in his bedroom at Kelmscott House.

Morris & Co.'s works at Merton Abbey. *Opposite above*, the wooden sheds standing on the banks of the river Wandle, which had previously been used for printing 'those hideous red and green table-cloths and so forth'. *Above*, the hand weaving looms used for making tapestries designed by Morris, Burne-Jones, Walter Crane and J. H. Dearle. *Right*, the dyeing vats, used for silk, wool and cotton. *Opposite, below*, Morris & Co.'s showroom at 449 Oxford Street, opened in 1877.

had exactly the right properties for use in the dyeing process. Pits were dug and lined to make indigo vats, and the sheds were turned into a dye house, a printing shop, a studio for painting glass and a weaving factory. For the first time the firm had facilities to produce its own tapestries and carpets and to print cotton chintzes and silks. Morris was delighted with the Merton Abbey works and spent three or four days a week there.

The products of Morris & Co. had by now become highly fashionable. In 1877 the firm opened showrooms in Oxford Street, in the heart of the West End of London. Morris wallpapers and fabrics attained the status of a cult among the wealthy upper classes. Moncure Conway noted in his travels through west London in 1882 that in the fashionable new Bedford Park estate 'the majority of the residents have used the wallpapers and designs of Morris'. The firm attracted an increasingly grand clientèle. In 1881 it was asked to carry out the redecoration of the throne room and reception rooms at St James's Palace, and in 1887 Morris produced a special wallpaper for Balmoral, Queen Victoria's new house in Scotland.

SPECIMENS OF
UPHOLSTERED
FURNITURE

MORRIS
AND
COMPANY
DECORATORS, LTD.
449 OXFORD STREET,
LONDON, W.
AND MERTON ABBEY, SURREY.

DECORATION

Design for flock wall-paper

MORRIS & COMPANY
449 Oxford Street W

Morris himself was very worried by this trend. There had always been a conflict between his ideal of reviving the simplicity and functionalism of medieval craftsmanship to produce beautiful and useful works of art for the people and the reality of the firm's fashionable image and wealthy clientèle. The original prospectus of Morris & Co. had promised that 'good decoration, involving rather the luxury of taste than the luxury of costliness, will be found to be much less expensive than is generally supposed'. But by the very nature of the elaborate processes that went into their manufacture, the firm's products were very expensive, and their customers only the well off. Morris found his role of pandering to the tastes of the haute-bourgeoisie increasingly distasteful. In 1876 Sir Lowthian Bell, a wealthy iron-master whose home the firm was decorating, asked Morris why he was pacing up and down the room muttering to himself. 'It's only that I spend my life in ministering to the swinish luxury of the rich,' was the curt reply.

Morris's growing unease about the disparity between his ideals and his actual work led him seriously to reconsider his attitudes to art and society during the late 1870s. He finally rejected the philosophy of art for art's sake and the lofty detachment from all contemporary concerns that he had, at least in part, imbibed from Rossetti. Instead he returned to the awareness of the social and economic forces that shape art which he had begun to perceive as an undergraduate as a result of his reading of Ruskin and Carlyle. This was eventually to lead him to the conclusion that it was impossible to have good art in the debased social and economic conditions of Late Victorian England. Initially, though, Morris's new contemporary awareness revealed itself in a complete change of attitude towards the restoration and 'medievalization' of old buildings.

During the Victorian Age the practice had grown up of rebuilding cathedrals and churches to make them individually uniform and consistent in style. The instigators of this development, the Cambridge Camden Society, believed that no building should be left as a collection of parts from different periods but should rather be rebuilt in one particular style. Morris was at first an avid supporter of this movement to 'restore' medieval churches, which found favour with such leading architects as Scott, Salvin, Bodley and Pearson. His own firm assisted in the 1860s in the restoration of three Cambridge colleges, and a third of the stained glass it produced before 1877 went into old churches. Extensive restoration was often the only way of saving dilapidated medieval churches from destruction and of freeing them of later accretions like box pews. But many architects went further than this in their passion for restoration, and actually rebuilt sound churches which displayed different architectural styles to restore them to their original state. Sir George Gilbert Scott pulled down the

Opposite, signs of Morris & Co.'s increasingly fashionable image: *above*, Bedford Park, the London garden suburb laid out by Norman Shaw in 1878, where most of the residents had Morris wallpapers. *Below left*, a catalogue of upholstered furniture issued by the firm in the 1880s. *Below right*, wallpaper designed by Morris for Balmoral, Queen Victoria's new Scottish residence, in 1887.

The east end of Oxford Cathedral before (*above*) and after (*above right*) restoration by Sir George Gilbert Scott in 1853. Scott destroyed the fourteenth-century east window and replaced it with his own late Norman wheel window, which he regarded as more in harmony with the rest of the building. It was this kind of 'restoration' that prompted Morris to set up the Society for the Protection of Ancient Buildings.

east wall of Oxford Cathedral and rebuilt it in the Norman style, because that was how it must originally have been.

In re-reading Ruskin's *Stones of Venice*, Morris realized the futility and illogicality of this mania for restoration. In his chapter 'On the Nature of Gothic' Ruskin stressed that it was the peculiar life style and aspirations of the medieval craftsmen that made Gothic architecture what it was. It could never be recreated in the totally different conditions of the nineteenth century. Each period had its own style of architecture that was valid for its own age. To attempt in one age to recreate the style of another was a bogus and fraudulent activity. Morris accepted the truth of this. 'The workman of today', he wrote, 'is not an artist as his forefather was; it is impossible, under his circumstances, that he could translate the work of the ancient handicraftsmen.' Old buildings should be preserved as they are, as monuments to the many talents that created them, rather than destroyed in an effort to reduce them to a sham uniformity of style.

During a drive through the Cotswolds towards the end of 1876 Morris was horrified to see alterations being made to Burford Church. Early the following year he read of proposals by Scott to 'restore'

Tewkesbury Abbey. A letter to the *Athenaeum* led to a meeting at the Morris & Co. showrooms in March 1877 at which it was decided to form a Society for the Protection of Ancient Buildings. The Society, which soon came to be known as 'Anti-Scrape', had distinguished supporters. Its original committee included Carlyle, Ruskin, Burne-Jones and Philip Webb, with Morris as secretary. From the moment of its inception, Morris & Co. refused all further commissions for making new stained-glass windows for old churches.

The influence and importance of the Society for the Protection of Ancient Buildings was considerable. Although the cause of preserving old buildings had been canvassed as far back as the 1790s, it had been swamped by the Victorian passion for restoration. Now in the Society's manifesto Morris put the clear case for conservation rather than restoration. Old buildings, he wrote, 'are not in any sense our property, to do as we like with them. We are only trustees for those that come after us.' The protests of the Society were instrumental in stopping schemes to add to Westminster Abbey and rebuild Westminster Hall, demolish the old school buildings at Eton, and pull down St Mary-le-Strand and St Mary-at-Hill churches in London. A campaign organized by Morris's old master Street and supported by Gladstone and Disraeli helped to prevent the rebuilding of the west front of St Mark's Cathedral, Venice. One of the Society's original committee members, the Liberal Member of Parliament, Sir John Lubbock, succeeded in 1882 in securing the Ancient Monuments Protection Act, the first legislative measure to protect important old buildings by providing for them to be taken into public ownership.

Morris's battles with both the ecclesiastical and the secular establishment in the course of his work as Secretary of the Society for the Protection of Ancient Buildings reinforced the conviction given him by his experience in the firm that the kind of art which a society produced was closely related to the balance of social and economic forces within it. In his own age he felt that it was commercialism that was ruining good art, and a taste for ornamentation and luxury that was destroying the simplicity of the best design. He developed these two themes in a series of lectures which he gave to working men, initially to raise funds for Anti-Scrape, between 1877 and 1885. It was in these lectures, published together in *Hopes and Fears of Art* in 1882, that Morris worked out the theory of art and society which was to be one of the most important components of his socialist philosophy.

At a practical level, Morris's lectures were a call to others to take up the traditional crafts which he himself had mastered and a guide to the techniques of pattern designing, weaving and dyeing. The emphasis, as in Morris's work, was on creating objects which were beautiful and useful. In his first lecture, *The Decorative Arts: their Relation to Modern*

Life and Progress, which was delivered on 4 December 1877 to the Trades' Guild of Learning, Morris described his subject as 'that great body of art, by means of which men have at all times more or less striven to beautify the familiar matters of everyday life . . . the crafts of house building, painting, joinery and carpentry, smiths' work, pottery and glass making, weaving and many others'. He went on to make a characteristic plea for utility and simplicity: 'To give people pleasure in things they must perforce *use*, that is one great office of decoration; to give people pleasure in the things they must perforce *make*, that is the other use of it. . . . Simplicity of life, begetting simplicity of taste, that is, a love for sweet and lofty things, is of all matters most necessary for the birth of the new and better art we crave for.'

Predictably, Morris's lectures dwelt much on the vulgarity of modern mass-produced art compared with the beauty of the products

Caricature by Burne-Jones of Morris giving a lecture on weaving. Morris often lectured on the practical aspects of art as well as on the theory.

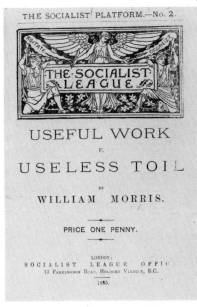

THE SOCIALIST PLATFORM.—No. 2.

THE·SOCIALIST
LEAGUE

USEFUL WORK
v.
USELESS TOIL

BY

WILLIAM MORRIS.

PRICE ONE PENNY.

LONDON:
SOCIALIST LEAGUE OFFIC
13 FARRINGDON ROAD, HOLBORN VIADUCT, E.C.
1885.

of the medieval craftsmen. In a lecture on *The Prospects for Architecture* in 1880, he contrasted the awful ugliness of the Victorian jerry-built house with the beauty of an ordinary yeoman's cottage built three hundred years before in a Cotswold village. The reason for the difference was not simply that one had been mass-produced and the other built by craftsmen. It lay rather in the different attitudes and situations of the workmen, and specifically in the control that they had over their materials and tools. Machines were all right provided that they saved hard labour and were used as the servants of the workman and not as his masters. Indeed, in a later lecture, *Useful Work versus Useless Toil*, Morris was to see a role for machines in reducing the average man's work to only four hours a day. What made the art of the Middle Ages so superior to the art of the nineteenth century was not the absence of machines but the greater independence and happiness of the workers. 'The chief source of art', Morris told one of his audiences,

William Morris, aged about 50, in the mid 1880s.

Useful Work versus Useless Toil (1885) in which Morris predicted that the machine would reduce man's work to four hours a day.

73

'is man's pleasure in his daily necessary work, which expresses itself and is embodied in that art itself. . . . The beauty of the handicrafts of the Middle Ages came from this: that the workman had control over his material, tools and time.' It was this dimension which was lacking from the life of the modern workman, turning out mass-produced artefacts for a weekly wage. It was small wonder that his products had the merits neither of utility nor of beauty. They lacked the sympathetic touch of the craftsman who, 'as he fashioned the thing under his hand, ornamented it so naturally and so entirely without conscious effort, that it is often difficult to distinguish where the more utilitarian part of his work ended and the ornamental began'.

This great attack on contemporary techniques of production and call to revive the craftsmanship of the Middle Ages inspired several young artists to follow Morris's example in the 1880s. The years following his lectures saw the birth of the Arts and Crafts Movement in Britain. Morris was not the sole inspiration for this movement. The first two societies set up for the promotion of artistic craftsmanship, Christopher Dresser's Art Furniture Alliance of 1880 and Arthur Mackmurdo's Century Guild of 1882, were largely independent of his influence. But part of the purpose of his lectures had been to stimulate others to set up ventures similar to his own firm and he played an active part in the foundation of at least two arts and crafts groups, the Art Workers' Guild in 1884, and the Arts and Crafts Exhibition Society which was established in 1886 to draw public attention 'to that really most important side of art, the decoration of utilities, by furnishing them with genuine artistic finish in place of trade finish'. Two years later C. R. Ashbee, who had been much impressed by Morris's lectures, set up his Guild and School of Handicraft.

Morris's lectures, however, were very much more than a call for a revival of the medieval tradition of craftsmanship, even if this was how they were interpreted by most of his audiences. They presented a biting attack not just on contemporary art, but on contemporary society. 'Apart from my desire to produce beautiful things,' Morris told one audience, 'the leading passion of my life is hatred of modern civilisation.' His lectures attacked the values and standards of Victorian society with a bitterness and vigour that were far removed from his image as a gentle romantic. 'Was it all to end in a counting house,' he thundered, 'on the top of a cinder heap, with Podsnap's drawing-room in the offing, and a Whig committee, dealing out champagne to the rich and margarine to the poor in such convenient proportions, as would make all men contented together, though the pleasures of the eyes have ever gone from the world, and the place of Homer was to be taken by Huxley.'

This savage attack on contemporary values in Morris's lectures derived from his central theory that art reflected the condition of the society which produced it. Since art was essentially the product of man's labour, it followed that it must reflect particularly closely the economic conditions in which it was created. And it was in economic factors that Morris found the explanation for the great difference between medieval and modern art. The artefacts of the Middle Ages were beautiful because they were made by independent craftsmen having control of their own means of production and working in trade guilds and associations. The Renaissance and the rise of capitalism destroyed this system of co-operation and substituted one of competition, based on the profit motive and the wage relationship. The quest for luxury and ostentation by rich capitalists replaced the medieval world's respect for plainness and simplicity. The Industrial Revolution further reduced the independence of workers, turning them into slaves to factory masters and machines. Modern works of art should be rejected not so much for themselves as for the sick society which could create them. 'It is not so much because the wretched thing is so ugly and silly and useless that I ask you to cast it from you,' Morris told the audience of one of his lectures, 'it is much more because these are but the outward symbols of the poison that lies within them; look through them and see all that has gone into their fashioning, and you will see how vain labour, and sorrow, and disgrace have been their companions from the first – and all this for trifles that no man really needs.'

The corollary to this argument was simple. Morris stated it in an article in 1885: 'When art is fairly in the clutch of profit-grinding she dies, and leaves behind her but her phantom of sham art as the futile slave of the capitalist. . . . Socialism is the only hope of the arts.' It was his conviction that good art could not come out of a society dedicated to profit where workers were exploited and alienated from the pleasures of their labour that first turned Morris towards socialism. He himself attributed his initial espousal of socialism to his awareness 'that art cannot have a real life and growth under the present system of commercialism and profit-mongering'.

Morris was helped along this rather unorthodox road to socialism by treading also a more familiar route. Like so many other middle-class socialists he came to espouse the creed at least partly from feelings of guilt. In a lecture in 1881 he told how he often reflected as he sat at his window in Hammersmith watching ruffians going past swearing and shouting outside, that:

it was my good luck only of being respectable and rich, that has put me on this side of the window among delightful books and lovely works of art, and not on the other side, in the empty street, the drink-steeped liquor shops, the foul and degraded lodgings. I know by my own feelings and desires what these men want, what would have saved them from this lowest depth of savagery: employment which would foster their self-respect and win the

Unemployed workers in the streets of
London, 1886, and *below*, Morris's
well-stocked library at Kelmscott
House, Hammersmith. He was very
concious of the disparity between his
own comfortable life-style and the
wretched existence endured by the
majority of the population.

praise and sympathy of their fellows, and dwellings which they could come to with pleasure, surroundings which would soothe and elevate them; reasonable labour and reasonable rest.

This profound sense of the injustice of a society which left him able to develop and enjoy himself freely but tied others to wage slavery underpinned Morris's socialist faith and gave it a strong moral character. His own definition of socialism indicates the nobility of his vision:

a condition of society in which there should be neither rich nor poor, neither master nor master's man, neither idle nor overworked, neither brain-sick workers nor heart-sick hand workers, in a word, in which all men would be living in equality of condition, and would manage their affairs unwastefully, and with full consciousness that harm to one would mean harm to all – the realisation at last of the meaning of the word 'Commonwealth'.

Morris's socialism, then, was based on his own theory of the relationship between art and society and on his moral sense. He had worked it out for himself. Until he joined the Democratic Federation in January 1883, he had not read the works of any other socialist writers. His only knowledge of socialist theory, in fact, came from a series of critical articles by John Stuart Mill in the *Fortnightly* in 1879. 'I was blandly ignorant of economics,' he later recalled, 'I had never so much as opened Adam Smith, or heard of Ricardo, or Karl Marx.' This last gap in Morris's knowledge was soon to be filled. By 1884 his copy of *Das Kapital* needed rebinding because of wear and tear. He found the book hard going. He enjoyed the historical chapters which confirmed his own view of the Middle Ages, but 'suffered agonies of confusion of the brain over reading the pure economics of that great work'. Economics was never to be Morris's strong point as a socialist. There was a celebrated occasion in December 1884 after he had been speaking in Glasgow when he was asked by a member of the audience whether he accepted Marx's theory of value. Morris replied, 'To speak quite frankly, I do not know what Marx's theory of value is, and I'm damned if I want to know! It's enough political economy for me to know that the idle class is rich and the working class is poor! And it doesn't matter a rap whether the robbery is accompanied by what is termed "surplus value" or by means of subterfuge or open brigandage.'

Morris was, in fact, being less than fair to himself on this occasion. He had understood and assimilated Marx's theory of surplus value and of the consequent alienation of workers in industrial society. Indeed, he regarded it as the central characteristic of the capitalist system. 'The creation of surplus value being the one aim of the employers of labour,' he later wrote, 'they cannot for a moment trouble themselves as to

Karl Marx (1818–83). Morris became one of Marx's leading British disciples, and went with a group of socialists to pay homage to his grave in March 1884. Denied access by the police, they adjourned and sang the *Internationale*.

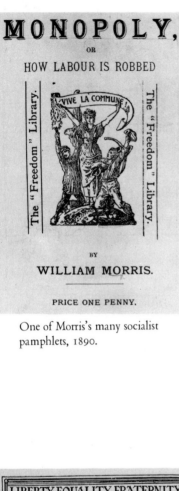

One of Morris's many socialist pamphlets, 1890.

The membership card which Morris designed for the Democratic Federation.

whether the work which creates that surplus value is pleasurable to the worker or not.' Marx's theory of alienation fitted exactly with Morris's views about the need for workmen to have control of their work and feel delight in what they were making. This, he felt, was impossible in capitalist society. It was not surprising that when Morris was asked to define his own political position, he described himself as a communist 'on the side of Karl Marx *contra mundum*'.

Morris also followed Marx in having a strong conviction of the importance of class conflict and revolution in bringing about a socialist society. Iceland had impressed him as a community which acted despite appalling poverty in a co-operative and socialistic way because of its absence of class divisions. In Britain the strength of the ruling and capitalist classes acted as a barrier to socialist development. Morris wrote to a friend in October 1883, 'I think the basis of all change must be the antagonism of classes ... commercialism, competition, has sown the wind recklessly, and must reap the whirlwind: it has created the proletariat for its own interest, and its creation will and must destroy it.' Morris saw the signs of such a revolt by the working classes of England in the early 1880s. If he had not believed in the possibility of imminent revolution, he would probably never have become a socialist, and would have continued to share the general complacency and contentment of the Victorian intelligentsia whom he came to despise. As it was, he explained later in his important article, *How I Became a Socialist* (1894):

The consciousness of revolution stirring amidst our hateful modern society prevented me, luckier than many others of artistic perceptions, from crystallising into a mere railer against progress, on the one hand, and on the other from wasting time and energy in any of the nervous schemes by which the quasi-artistic of the middle classes hope to make art grow when it has no longer any root, and thus I became a practical Socialist.

Morris lost no time in throwing himself into practical socialist politics once he had worked out his own theoretical position. In the summer of 1882, only a few months after he had resigned as treasurer of the National Liberal League, he declared himself ready 'to join any body who distinctly called themselves Socialists'. The following January he enlisted in the ranks of the only genuinely socialist organization in Britain, the Democratic Federation, which had been set up in 1881 by Henry Mayers Hyndman. By the summer of 1883 he was on the Federation's executive and was addressing street-corner meetings. In January 1884, when the Federation changed its name to the Social Democratic Federation, he was out on the streets selling its new weekly paper, *Justice*. He quickly dispelled any worries that his socialist colleagues might have had about his commitment to the cause. One of them had expressed his misgivings when Morris first

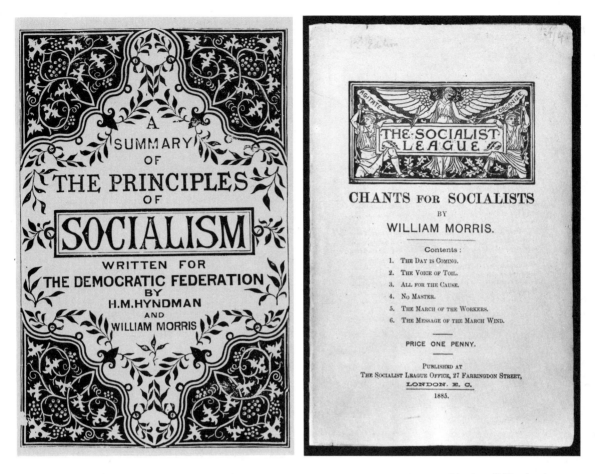

joined the Federation: 'All we knew about him was that he kept a highly select shop in Oxford Street where he sold furniture of a rum aesthetic sort and decorated houses with extraordinary colours.' But soon Hyndman was commenting that he was 'even too eager to take his full share in the unpleasant part of our public work and to show that he meant to work in grim earnest on the same level as the rank and file of our party'. The two men collaborated in producing a sixty-four-page *Summary of the Principles of Socialism* in the spring of 1884. Morris contributed frequent articles to *Justice*, including a series of 'Chants for Socialists'. Meanwhile he continued his lectures around the country on art and its relationship to society. In March 1883 he delivered his first lecture since becoming an active socialist at the Manchester Royal Institution. His subject was *Art, Wealth and Riches*, and he surprised his audience by his furious denunciation of capitalism. The following November he caused even more of a stir by calling for recruits to the socialist movement in a lecture to undergraduates at University College, Oxford. He had been invited by the dons to talk on art as a

In 1884 Morris and Hyndman wrote *A Summary of the Principles of Socialism* for the emerging socialist movement in Britain.

Morris's *Chants for Socialists* were to become staple fare at early Labour Party gatherings and socialist Sunday School concerts.

Friedrich Engels (1820–95), photographed c. 1890. He hoped Morris would lead a socialist revolution in Britain, but regarded him as too sentimental and unpractical.

Philip Webb (1831–1915), painted in 1873 by Charles Fairfax Murray. A lifelong friend of Morris, and principal furniture designer for his firm, Webb was one of the few people to follow him into the socialist camp.

fellow academic, having been elected at the beginning of the year to an honorary fellowship at Exeter College. They had overlooked the fact that on the day of his election he had also joined the Democratic Federation, 'Hyndman's congregation of manual working pseudo-Marxists', as Bernard Shaw described it.

In becoming an active socialist in the early 1880s, Morris cut himself off from the artistic world in which he had previously moved. No longer was he the harmless medievalist and romantic whose designs and poems were so popular in Victorian drawing-rooms. He had suddenly become a rather threatening figure, preaching revolution and attacking the existing order of things with a ferocity that seemed far removed from the gentle patterns of his wallpapers and the dreamy verses of *The Earthly Paradise*. Of the close circle of friends which he had kept since Oxford and Pre-Raphaelite days, only Philip Webb and Charles Faulkner followed him into the socialist camp. Swinburne and de Morgan, who had supported him over the Eastern Question, politely excused themselves from joining him in what they took to be

May Morris with her husband, Henry Halliday Sparling and, on the right, Steffan, a Swedish economist, and his wife.

this new aberration. His closest friends, Edward and Georgiana Burne-Jones, could never understand what had taken him into a movement which they regarded as sour and bitter, and which they blamed for destroying his sense of humour. Nor could his wife Jane, who always avoided his new socialist friends when he brought them home. The only member of Morris's family to follow her father's new faith was his younger daughter, May, who was later to marry Henry Sparling, a prominent member of the Socialist League.

Morris exchanged his old artistic friends for a new group of political colleagues. He became one of the circle of progressive left-wing thinkers which was establishing itself in London in the early 1880s. It included a number of exiles from the Continent: the romantic Prince Peter Kropotkin who had escaped to England in 1876 after being arrested for anarchist activities in his native Russia; Andreas Scheu, who had fled from persecution in Vienna for his socialist writings in 1874; Frank Kitz, who was born in England of German parents and settled in Soho in the 1870s where he founded the Manhood Suffrage League, and Friedrich Engels, the German businessman who had come to England in 1842 and subsequently worked with Karl Marx on the Communist Manifesto. All four men were to become close associates of Morris. Among his companions on the Executive of the Social Democratic Federation were Marx's daughter, Eleanor, and her future husband Edward Aveling, the scientist and freethinker; Annie Besant, the feminist and secularist who later became converted to theosophy; Charles Bradlaugh, whose atheist principles led him to be refused entry into the House of Commons for six years after he had

Eleanor Marx, photographed c. 1880. She wanted to be an actress, but her marriage to Edward Aveling led her to take an active part in the socialist movement.

Henry Mayers Hyndman, founder of the Democratic Federation (on left). Engels described him as 'a political adventurer and Parlimentary careerist'.

Caricature by Burne-Jones indicating Morris's love of good living.

been elected as an MP; Belfort Bax, the socialist and ethical philosopher; and Hyndman himself, who had been converted to socialism in a meeting with Marx.

The Burne-Joneses were right in regarding these new friends as much more serious than the company Morris had previously been accustomed to keep. The early socialists did not have the Pre-Raphaelite taste for practical jokes. Their attitudes and behaviour were certainly avant-garde: in their repudiation of marriage and their open disavowal of all religious belief they deliberately flew in the face of conventional Victorian morality. But they were in deadly earnest about their business. Morris undoubtedly lost some of his gaiety in their company. From now on his life was to be devoted first and foremost to writing and lecturing to promote the socialist cause and only secondly to his art and poetry. Not that he gave up the latter pursuits entirely, by any means. On train journeys to his lectures across the country in the 1880s he occupied himself with a translation of Homer's *Odyssey* which was published in 1887. In spare moments between political meetings he worked out new designs for wallpapers and textiles. He still managed to visit the firm's works at Merton at reasonably frequent intervals. But all these activities were now subordinate to his main task of forwarding the socialist revolution.

For all Morris's socialist pronouncements, he continued to live the life of a capitalist, enjoying the profits of his firm and employing his workers for a fixed wage just like the factory masters whom he attacked so virulently. His own lifestyle was comfortably bourgeois. He continued to the end of his life to maintain his spacious country retreat at Kelmscott as well as his house in London which was well equipped with servants. Morris was conscious of the inconsistency between what he practised and what he preached, but he did not do very much about it. At one stage he thought of joining the proletariat by selling the firm and living on a weekly wage, and he also toyed with the idea of involving his workers in a profit sharing co-operative. But he decided against it on the grounds that profit sharing merely turned the workers into small capitalists, and that the profits of Morris & Co. were anyway too small to be adequately shared around. He told Georgiana Burne-Jones rather feebly: 'I am not a capitalist, I am a hanger-on of that class like all professional men.'

Morris was also conscious that while he called for art for all the people, his firm continued to supply it only to the few. Throughout the 1880s and early 1890s, while their manager was denouncing the upper classes and the capitalist system, Morris & Co. decorated the houses of the aristocracy and the very rich, like Clouds in Wiltshire which had been designed by Philip Webb for Percy Wyndham, the younger son of Lord Leconfield, and Wightwick Manor in Shropshire, built by Edward Ould for Theodore Mander, a successful paint and varnish

The Morning Room at Clouds, near East Knoyle, Wiltshire, built by Webb between 1880 and 1886 for a leading political family and frequented by the Balfours, the Curzons and the Londonderrys. It shows how much more sophisticated he had become since designing Red House. The foreground carpet and loose covers are by Morris.

The Great Parlour, Wightwick Manor, Shropshire. Built between 1887 and 1893, it provided Morris & Co. with one of their grandest commissions. The decoration of the Parlour is 'an epitome of the artistic taste of the 1890s, with blue and white china in cupboards across the walls, a great frieze under the roof of Orpheus and Eurydice, and a multitude of hangings, embroideries and coverings from the Morris workshops'.

manufacturer. Morris never really attempted to overcome the problem that the kind of products he made were far too expensive to become popular. He never designed genuinely cheap art for mass consumption. The only constructive suggestion that he made on the subject was in an interview in the *Daily Chronicle* in 1893, when he said that in a socialist state tapestries would become public property and would be hung on the walls of town halls for all to enjoy. Otherwise, he pinned his hopes on the great and cheap works of art that would be created, and appreciated naturally by the people in the coming socialist Utopia.

Early on in his socialist career Morris found himself at the centre of one of those fierce quarrels over ideology and tactics which bedevil left-wing political movements. Hyndman favoured turning the Social Democratic Federation, which had made considerable headway in 1883 and 1884, into an orthodox political party which would campaign for specific reforms and put up candidates at local and parliamentary elections. Morris, with others of the Executive, was unhappy at the compromises which this would inevitably involve. His own experiences with the Liberals had made him disillusioned with Parliament, which he regarded as an essential part of the capitalist system which socialists must destroy. He felt that Hyndman's proposed strategy of campaigning for specific reforms would simply play into the hands of their opponents, who would buy them off with small concessions. It was also unrealistic: the demand for an eight-hour working day, which Hyndman had suggested the Federation make its first campaign, was, said Morris, 'good as a cry, but how can a bourgeois government ever think of that?' He believed that there was going to be a revolution. In this situation, the job of socialists was not to join in the existing charade of party politics, but to educate the people for change. As Morris put it in an interview with the *Daily News*:

My belief is that the old order can only be overthrown by force; and for that reason it is all the more important that the revolution should not be an ignorant, but an educated revolution. What I should like to have now would be a body of able, high-minded, competent men who should act as instructors of the masses and as their leaders.

It was with this end in mind that Morris broke away from the Social Democratic Federation in December 1884 and set up his own Socialist League. He took with him ten members of the Federation's Executive, including Eleanor Marx, Edward Aveling and Belfort Bax. Morris announced to the opening meeting of the new body, 'Education towards Revolution seems to me to express in three words what our policy should be.' The League's executive echoed this in its first statement, which declared that it had 'no function but to educate

the people in the principles of Socialism, and to organise such as it can get hold of to take their due places, when the crisis shall come which shall force action upon us'. The Socialist League adopted a policy of complete non-participation in parliamentary politics. It distributed leaflets during elections calling on people to abstain from voting. Its role was entirely educational and propagandist. In February 1885 a weekly paper, *The Commonweal*, was started with Morris as editor, and in July of the same year a manifesto was issued which had been written by Morris and Belfort Bax. It began:

We come before you as a body advocating the principles of Revolutionary International Socialism: that is, we seek a change in the basis of society – a change which would destroy the distinctions of classes and nationalities.

Morris was emerging as one of the foremost proponents of revolutionary communism in Britain. In the manifesto of the Socialist League he looked forward to 'the time when any definite exchange will have entirely ceased to exist; just as it never existed in that primitive communism which preceded civilisation'. By the mid-1880s

The Hammersmith Branch of the Socialist League. In the front row May Morris is second from the left and Jenny Morris is fourth from the left. William Morris is fifth from the right in the middle row.

he had come to feel that that time was not far off. In October 1885 he wrote to Georgiana Burne-Jones:

One must turn to hope, and only in one direction do I see it – on the road to Revolution: everything else is gone now. And now at last when the corruption of society seems complete, there is arising a definite conception of a new order.

There was no doubt that Britain looked closer to revolution in the mid-1880s than it had done since the hungry forties and the days of the Chartists. A bad trade recession, which marked the end of the Victorian economic boom and of Britain's pre-eminence as an industrial and commercial power, brought high unemployment and severe distress. Disgruntled workers took to the streets of London and formed a ready audience for the rapidly growing band of socialist agitators and street-corner orators. On 20 September 1885 a mob variously estimated at between one and seven thousand jeered and jostled as the police arrested six socialist speakers for obstruction at the corner of Dod Street and Burdett Road in Limehouse, where the Social Democratic Federation had held regular open-air meetings for several months. The following morning Morris was among the visitors in the magistrates' court who heard a sentence of two months' hard labour being given to one of the speakers. This severity provoked an uproar in the courtroom during which Morris was accused of breaking a policeman's helmet. He was brought before the magistrates but allowed to go free after replying in answer to a question about his identity: 'I am an artistic and literary man, pretty well known, I think, throughout Europe.'

The atmosphere of agitation in London continued throughout 1886. In February, following a rally of the Social Democratic Federation in Trafalgar Square, an angry crowd marched through the West End smashing the windows of clubs and looting shops. Morris & Co.'s showrooms in Oxford Street were only just spared from damage by the staff's prompt action in putting up the shutters. The police made numerous arrests at subsequent open-air socialist rallies, and Morris was frequently present in courtrooms standing bail for his friends. His own privileged position in the eyes of the authorities was revealed again in July 1886 when, after deliberately courting arrest by obstructing the highway during a meeting in the Edgware Road, he was fined only one shilling when one of his companions was sent to prison for two months. The magistrate even apologized for fining him, and politely told him that 'as a gentleman, he would at once see, when it was pointed out to him, that such meetings were a nuisance, and would desist from taking part in them'.

Morris was encouraged by what he took to be these stirrings of the revolutionary spirit to continue rejecting the reformist, parliamentary

The mob in St James's Street, London, February 1886. Following a rally of the Social Democratic Federation an angry crowd went on the rampage through the West End.

'The Attitude of the Police', a cartoon of 1886 commenting on the lenient attitude taken by the authorities towards Morris when he committed offences. A policeman with tears in his eyes is polishing Morris's boots at the corner of Dod Street, where the Social Democratic Federation often held meetings and there were frequent arrests for obstruction.

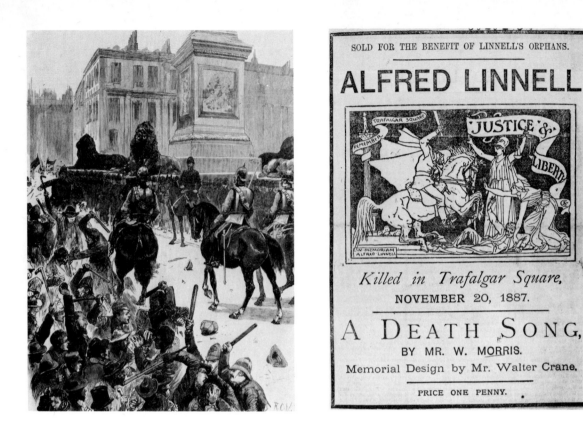

Above, the riots in Trafalgar Square on 'Bloody Sunday', 13 November 1887. Morris said he had 'not realised till that day how soon a scratch body of men could be scattered by a comparatively small but well-organised force'. *Above right*, Morris's *Death Song* for Alfred Linnell, killed following another riot a week later.

road to socialism. At a conference of the Socialist League in May 1887 he won the day over those who advocated working through Parliament and using the existing political system. But the revolution showed no signs of coming. Quite the reverse in fact. The brutal suppression by the police of a demonstration in Trafalgar Square on 13 November called by the Law and Liberty League, which had been formed on Morris's suggestion to defend the right of free speech, showed how strong were the forces of authority and how meekly the people succumbed to them. The ease and savagery with which this demonstration was put down, which caused the day on which it occurred to be dubbed 'Bloody Sunday', saddened and depressed Morris, as did the death of a young man, Alfred Linnell, from injuries inflicted by the police when quelling a demonstration the following week. He had always hoped and believed that revolution would come both quickly and peacefully. Although he optimistically entitled his first collection of socialist essays published in 1888 *Signs of Change*, it was now rapidly becoming clear to him that revolution was still a long way off and that, even if it did come, it would inevitably involve bloodshed.

Further disillusionment set in when Morris attended the Second International Socialist Workingmen's Congress in Paris in July 1889. He had been selected by the international committee to present the report on the progress of the socialist movement in England, with Keir Hardie, the Scottish miners' leader, giving a report on the parliamentary side of the movement. This was a sign of the extent to which Morris was by now recognized in Europe as the leader of British socialism. But he was disappointed that the International became bogged down in factiousness. It spent most of its time discussing whether it should or should not merge with a rival congress which had been set up by French advocates of the parliamentary approach to socialism, with the strong support of Hyndman. He was further discouraged when the European Marxists at the International passed resolutions in favour of gradual reforms like the Eight Hour Working Day against which he had campaigned in Britain. They also seemed to have little faith in revolution.

Meanwhile Morris's defeat of the parliamentarians in the Socialist League had pushed it into the hands of anarchists. In June 1890 he was ejected from the editorship of *The Commonweal* and replaced by Frank Kitz and D.J. Nicoll, who wrote editorials calling for immediate armed insurrection and advocating the use of dynamite. A small group of anarchists captured the Executive Council of the League leaving Morris and Philip Webb isolated. In November Morris withdrew his own Hammersmith Branch, 120 strong, from the League and reconstituted it as the Hammersmith Socialist Society. The manifesto of this new society rejected both parliamentary socialism and anarchism, and declared that its object would be 'the spreading of the principles of Socialism, especially by Lectures, Street meetings, and Publications . . . and that object only'.

Morris's departure from the Socialist League really marked the end of his active involvement in socialism and the fading of his hopes that it would soon come about through a revolutionary struggle. For the last six years of his life he stood detached from the day-to-day battles, and tried vainly to promote unity between the divided socialist groups. In 1893 he organized an afternoon tea-party to bring together members of his own society, the Social Democratic Federation, and the Fabian Society which had been started in 1884 by Bernard Shaw and Sidney Webb. As a result *The Manifesto of English Socialists* was issued in May 1893. It at least united these three disparate groups behind a common programme, but it was little more than a collection of bland platitudes. Morris never wholly gave up his belief that a truly socialist society would only come through revolution. In 1895, the year before he died, he wrote: 'I have thought the matter up and down and in and out, and I cannot for the life of me see how the great change which we long for can come otherwise than by disturbance and suffering of some kind.'

Characteristically, Morris interpreted the concern with political tactics and narrow economic goals which he saw as preoccupying the socialist movement in the last decade of his life as a loss of idealism and moral vision. In his valedictory article in *The Commonweal* in November 1890, entitled 'Where Are We Now?', he wrote:

When we first began to work together there was little said about anything save the great ideals of socialism, and so far off did we seem from the realisation of these that we could hardly think of any means for their realisation . . . but now our very success has dimmed the great ideals and we have fallen into political methods and subterfuges.

Morris was too much of a purist to have any serious influence on the course of British politics. 'Our business', he wrote in his final *Commonweal* article, 'is the making of Socialists. We Socialists can do nothing else that is useful . . . preaching and teaching . . . are the only means of attaining to the New Order of Things.' Preaching and teaching, however, are not enough to effect fundamental political change. Socialism, in Morris's sense, was never achieved in Britain. The growth of a powerful movement of organized labour, through the rise of the trade unions and the Labour Party, was a poor substitute, which involved the political methods and subterfuges he so despised.

Morris's purism led him to reject, at least until the very end of his life, those organizations and methods by which the Labour movement in Britain was being advanced. He despised the social democracy of Hyndman and the Social Democratic Federation, the state socialism and reformism of the Fabians, which he dismissed as 'gas and water socialism', and the economic demands of the emerging trade union movement. All these groups, he felt, were accepting the basic premises of capitalist society and merely trying to tinker with it to alleviate its worst excesses. He wrote, 'I think the aim of Socialists should be the founding of a religion, towards which end compromise is no use, and we only want to have those with us who will be with us to the end.' In this spirit Morris dismissed the Fabians' campaign to win control of the London County Council for their Progressive Party and the foundation of the Independent Labour Party by Keir Hardie and others in 1893 as 'the wearisome shilly-shally of parliamentary politics'. He was less dismissive of the national dockers' strike in the summer of 1889 which marked the rise of the new unskilled trade unionism. 'However it ends,' he wrote of the strike in *The Commonweal*, 'it will have been the most important one of our times,' although he went on to indicate that he still saw it as something apart from the socialist movement, pointing out that 'mere combination amongst men, with no satisfactory ulterior aim, is not itself Socialism.'

It was, of course, through the election of Labour candidates to local government and Parliament and through the growth of trade unionism that the working classes began to achieve political and economic power at the end of the nineteenth century. Morris ultimately had to accept this, and indeed in the last three years of his life he appeared several times on Social Democratic Federation platforms and supported efforts to put socialists into Parliament. But he continued to believe that in the end men would take the revolutionary road to socialism. After Sidney Webb had given a lecture to the Hammersmith Socialist Society in October 1895, Morris said to him, 'The world is going your way at present, Webb, but it is not the right way in the end.'

One of the reasons why the world did not go Morris's way was undoubtedly his failure to strike a chord with ordinary working men, on whom he saw revolution depending. He always hoped that a proper working-class socialist leader would emerge, but one who shared his ideals and vision rather than a narrow trade unionist or politician. It was an unrealistic dream. As a revolutionary socialist from a bourgeois background, Morris had nothing in common with the working classes. His highflown theories about art and society left his audiences puzzled and unmoved. After a meeting in Stepney he admitted, 'it is a great drawback that I can't talk to them roughly and unaffectedly'. The truth was that working people were far more interested in the specific material rewards and the concrete reforms being fought for by trade unions and the Labour representatives in Parliament than they were in Morris's vague revolutionary ideals and his moral vision of a communist commonwealth. Perhaps the reaction would have been different if he had been putting his ideas across in the 1860s and 1870s, when the generally high level of prosperity in the country allowed people to indulge in political idealism, and to respond to Gladstone's moral crusades on behalf of the oppressed in distant corners of the world. But in the 1880s and early 1890s, the severe economic recession meant that the masses were predominantly interested in where their next job, or their next meal, was coming from, and had little time for the luxury of sharing the moral visions of a revolutionary socialist. Morris complained, 'the frightful ignorance and want of impressibility of the average English workman floors me at times'. But he was understanding enough to admit that 'If I were to work ten hours a day at work I despised and hated, I should spend my leisure, I hope, in political agitation, but, I fear, in drinking.'

Although Morris failed to attract any sizeable following among working men, he did build up a faithful body of young disciples. Most of them were of a literary or artistic bent, and were probably more attracted by his romantic appearance as an Old Testament prophet and his fame as a poet and designer than by his revolutionary socialist theories. Nonetheless they came regularly to the political meetings held every Sunday evening in the coach-house at Hammersmith and were

Morris in the 1880s, painted by
W.B. Richmond.

ready to help 'the cause' in whatever way they could. Walter Crane
offered his services as designer and engraver to the socialist movement,
and was a frequent contributor to *The Commonweal*. Emery Walker,
who was much involved in the Arts and Crafts Exhibition Society
and was later to help Morris with the Kelmscott Press, was secretary of
both the Hammersmith Branch of the Socialist League and the
Hammersmith Socialist Society. Others of Morris's young disciples
helped him in his personal rather than his political life. From
cataloguing Morris's library at Hammersmith, Sydney Cockerell was
promoted to be his private secretary and also to be secretary of the
Kelmscott Press. The young poet W.B. Yeats, although no sym-
pathizer with Morris's socialist ideas, became a close friend and
support to him after their first chance meeting in the street when Morris
had stopped him to say 'You write my sort of poetry.' He would have
said more, Yeats later recalled, 'had he not caught sight of a new
ornamental cast-iron lamp-post and got very heated upon the subject.'

Morris was disappointed that so few of his young disciples became
converted to his own brand of revolutionary socialism. He was also

'Rossetti's name is heard in America', cartoon by Max Beerbohm of Oscar Wilde lecturing with a lily in his hand. Morris had no time for this aspect of the Aesthetic Movement.

distressed at the rather precious quality many of them displayed both in their work and their thought. The excesses of the Arts and Crafts Movement were a constant embarrassment to him. T. J. Cobden-Sanderson, the book-binder, recalled a conversation in which Morris shocked him by saying, 'book-binding should be "rough"; did not want to multiply the minor arts: went so far as to suggest that some · machinery should be invented to bind books'. Nor did Morris have any sympathy for the namby-pambyism of the Aesthetic Movement of the 1880s and 1890s, to which several of his disciples belonged. He described its chief exponent, Oscar Wilde, as 'an ass', although his hostility was a little abated when Wilde produced an article on 'The Soul of Man Under Socialism' in 1891, possibly having been influenced by his attendance at the Hammersmith Sunday evening lectures.

The socialist gatherings organized by Morris at the coach-house in Hammersmith attracted an overwhelmingly cultured and bourgeois clientèle. They were not calculated to appeal to the less refined tastes of the proletariat. There were frequent 'Art Evenings' at which Morris

Annie Besant (1847–1933),
photographed in 1885. Pioneer
socialist and feminist, she hurled
herself bodily at the police cordons
on 'Bloody Sunday'.

and Edward Aveling read poems and Bernard Shaw played piano
duets with Annie Besant. Morris's *Chants For Socialists* were set to
music and sung by the choir of the Hammersmith Branch of the Social
Democratic Federation, which was under the direction of Gustav
Holst, a near neighbour of Morris. The Sunday evening lectures were
as likely to be on artistic or literary subjects as on politics or economics.
The same was true of Morris's articles in *Justice* or *The Commonweal*. He
would often devote considerable space to a review of the latest Royal
Academy Exhibition or a consideration of the saga form in Norse
literature.

It was not surprising that Engels should dismiss Morris as a
'sentimental Socialist' and an 'untalented politician'. Morris was
certainly no politician; he failed to see the importance of building up a
power base in organized labour to advance the socialist movement. He
was certainly sentimental, although he had a strong streak of realism as
well. When after one of his lectures a member of the audience asked for
his advice on decorating kitchens, he replied that a flitch of bacon
hanging from the ceiling would do very well. Perhaps 'medieval' is a
better word than 'sentimental' to describe Morris's socialism. It was

ORIGINAL CAST.

DRAMATIS PERSONÆ.—PART I.

Mr. La-di-da (*found guilty of swindling*)	H. BARTLETT.
Mr. Justice Nupkins...	W. BLUNDELL.
Mr. Hungary, Q.C. (*Counsel for the Prosecution*)...	W. H. UTLEY.
Sergeant Sticktoit (*Witness for Prosecution*) ...	JAMES ALLMAN.
Constable Potlegoff (*Witness for Prosecution*) ...	H. B. TARLETON.
Constable Strongithoath (*Witness for Prosecution*)	J. FLOCKTON.
Mary Pinch (*a labourer's wife, accused of theft*) ...	MAY MORRIS.
Foreman of Jury	T. CANTWELL.
Jack Freeman (*a Socialist, accused of conspiracy, sedition, and obstruction of the highway*)	H. H. SPARLING.
Archbishop of Canterbury (*Witness for Defence*)	W. MORRIS.
Lord Tennyson (*Witness for Defence*)	A. BROOKES.
Professor Tyndall (*Witness for Defence*)	H. BARTLETT.
William Joyce (*a Socialist Ensign*)	H. A. BARKER.
Usher	J. LANE.
Clerk of the Court	J. TURNER.

Jurymen, Interrupters, Revolutionists, etc., etc.

Opposite, the Coach House, Kelmscott House, Hammersmith. It was used for weaving carpets by day and, in the evenings, for socialist lectures and meetings. *Left*, Morris's only play, *The Tables Turned*, was performed there on 15 October 1887, with the author playing the part of the Archbishop of Canterbury.

rooted in a deep and original historical consciousness, best expressed in *Socialism: Its Growth and Outcome* which he wrote together with Belfort Bax and which was published in 1893. In this work, which reversed the prevailing liberal theme of progress, Morris expounded his historical theory of the progressive decay of cultures caused by the residuum from the last civilization infecting the new one. The Ancient World, based on slavery, gave way to the modern, which also ultimately became infected with economic and artistic slavery while attaining civil and political liberty. The only healthy civilization was the intervening one of the Middle Ages, where society was founded on the principles of association and co-operation, before decline set in with the Renaissance and then the Industrial Revolution.

Morris was realist enough to appreciate that there could be no simple return to the Middle Ages:

We cannot turn our people back into Catholic English peasants and Guild craftsmen, or into heathen Norse bonders, much as may be said for such conditions of life: we have no choice but to accept the task which the centuries have laid on us of using the corruption of three hundred years of profit-mongering for the overthrow of that very corruption.

He predicted a new commercial revolution in which gigantic commercial and industrial enterprises would replace small businesses and the bourgeoisie would cease to exist. With the middle classes absorbed into the proletariat, the way would be open for revolution.

Yet it is the theme of medievalism which predominates in the five great poetry and prose romances which Morris wrote between 1885 and 1890, and which are perhaps his greatest contribution to the development of socialism in Britain. These works share the lazy dream-like style and the escapist theme of *The Earthly Paradise*. Only one of them, *The Pilgrims of Hope*, deals with a modern subject and faces contemporary problems. The others are set in the remote past or the future. All stress the medieval values of community and kinship which Morris saw as so infinitely preferable to the worship of individualism of his own age.

The Pilgrims of Hope was the first of Morris's socialist romances. It consists of a collection of separate poems which initially appeared in monthly instalments in *The Commonweal* between March 1885 and July 1886. It is basically a love story set at the time of the Paris Commune and it treats such contemporary themes as wage slavery, unemployment and jingoism. The hero, after losing his wife to his best friend, becomes a revolutionary socialist and goes through many adventures, including being arrested after an open-air meeting. It is obviously autobiographical, and includes a revealing account of a speaker addressing a Radical club which shows his own frustration and despair:

> He spoke, were it well, were it ill, as though a message he bore,
> A word that he could not refrain from many a million men . . .
> But they sat and made no sign, and two of the glibber kind
> Stood up to jeer and to carp, his fiery words to blind.
> . . . I rose ere the meeting was done,
> And gave him my name and my faith – and I was the only one.

The Dream of John Ball appeared in serial form in *The Commonweal* from November 1886 to January 1887. Set against the background of the Peasants' Revolt, it was a hymn in praise of the brotherhood and fellowship of the Middle Ages. In Morris's words, its theme was:

the struggle against tyranny for the freedom of life, how that the wildwood and the heath, despite of wind and weather, were better for a free man than the court and the cheaping-town; of the taking from the rich to give to the poor; of the life of a man doing his own will and not the will of another man commanding him for the commandment's sake.

The House of the Wolfings, published in December 1888, and *The Roots of the Mountains*, published in November 1889, were based on Icelandic sagas. Both concern the adventures of Germanic tribes and

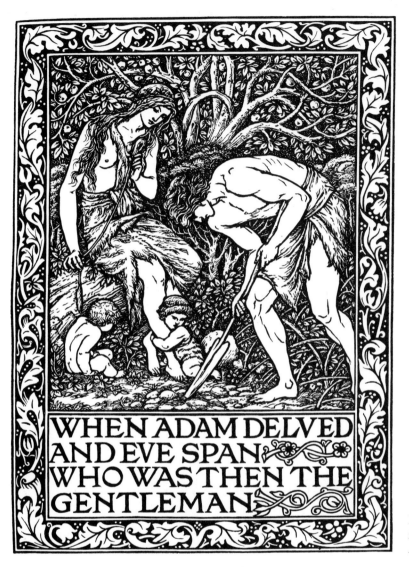

WHEN ADAM DELVED
AND EVE SPAN
WHO WAS THEN THE
GENTLEMAN

Burne-Jones's engraving for the 1892 illustrated edition of *A Dream of John Ball*.

stress the value of kinship and community. *The House of the Wolfings* is the story of a Gothic tribe with a strongly organized communal society, coming into conflict with Roman invaders bringing slavery, class divisions and a lust for money and power. It is a clear working-out of Morris's view of history, designed, as he put it, 'to illustrate the melting of the individual into the community'.

The greatest of Morris's socialist romances, *News From Nowhere*, was serialized in *The Commonweal* from January to October 1890. It is a Utopian tract which ranks with such other classics in this genre as Sir Thomas More's *Utopia* and Francis Bacon's *New Atlantis*. It portrays Britain in the twenty-first century as an ideal communist

Morris and Burne-Jones,
photographed c. 1890.

society which has ceased to worship production and become a
craftsman's paradise following a revolution in 1952. Morris actually
wrote *News From Nowhere* as a counter to a Fabian tract called *Looking
Backward*. This described the Fabians' ideal socialist society in which
everyone was graded and directed to work at a particular task and
where technology ruled supreme. Morris's Utopia, in contrast, is
libertarian, and machines are used only to do essential but disagreeable
or boring tasks. Work which is both inessential and unpleasant has
ceased, and all human labour has, therefore, become a source of
pleasure. It is a society of absolute equality, leading to a static balance

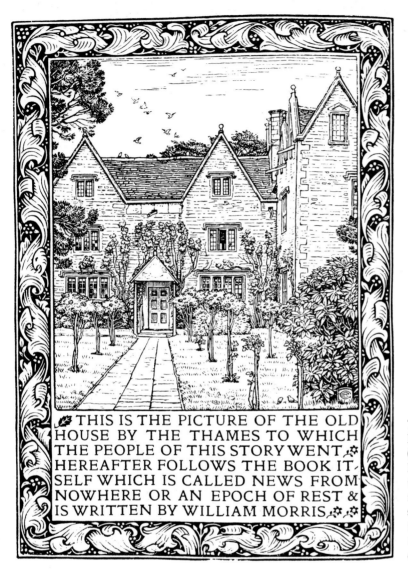

THIS IS THE PICTURE OF THE OLD HOUSE BY THE THAMES TO WHICH THE PEOPLE OF THIS STORY WENT. HEREAFTER FOLLOWS THE BOOK ITSELF WHICH IS CALLED NEWS FROM NOWHERE OR AN EPOCH OF REST & IS WRITTEN BY WILLIAM MORRIS.

The frontispiece of the Kelmscott Press edition of *News From Nowhere* (1892), based on the east front of Kelmscott Manor. The travellers in the book arrive at the end at 'this many-gabled old house built by the simple country folks of the long past times, regardless of all the turmoil that was going on in cities and courts'.

of supply and demand, and with the profit motive banished there is no temptation to manufacture and advertise useless and superflous goods. People make things because they want to, and because they are needed, and for no other reason.

Like so much of Morris's best writing, *News From Nowhere* harks back to the rural society of the Middle Ages. 'England was once a country of clearings amongst the woods and forests,' the narrator who wakes up out of a dream to find himself in the twenty-first century is told, 'it then became a country of huge and foul workshops . . . it is now a garden, where nothing is wasted and nothing spoilt.' This is thanks to a great urban clearance and tree-planting programme in 1955 which followed hard on the heels of the revolution. There is no mention of factories. Indeed there has been a return to manual labour with men cheerfully building and repairing roads with their hands. The Houses of Parliament are used for storing dung, since there is no need for politics any more. The society portrayed is simple, static and blissfully happy. It is medieval in even the smallest details. The costume worn by the women, for example, is 'somewhat between that of the ancient classical costume and the simpler forms of the fourteenth century garments'.

In 1891 Morris embarked on his last artistic project, the printing and binding of fine books. Once again the medieval influence was strong. He had long admired the illuminated manuscripts of the Middle Ages, and the work of Caxton and other early printers. The book appealed to him as an art-form – it was a necessary everyday article which yet 'had a tendency to be a beautiful object'. For some time he had wanted to produce books of a finer quality than those produced by contemporary publishers and printers, with their dull, pinched type and poor-quality bindings. In 1888 he was stimulated into action by a lecture on book design by Emery Walker, and by examples of new typography in the Arts and Crafts Exhibition. He personally supervised the printing of *The House of the Wolfings* in a type which he had originally chosen for an abortive illustrated edition of *The Earthly Paradise* twenty years before. In the summer of 1890 Morris decided to set up his own printing and publishing firm to produce fine editions of classic works. He set to work designing a new typeface, installed three Albion presses in a cottage a few doors away from his house in Hammersmith, and took on a retired master printer and two assistants to work them. On 12 January 1891 the Kelmscott Press was ready for business.

Fifty-three titles were produced by the Kelmscott Press during its seven years of operation. Morris designed nearly all of them himself. He tried to make his books look as much as possible like medieval manuscripts or early printed works, and made considerable use of ornamental initials and borders. He designed two typefaces, the 'Golden', a heavy Roman style based on the work of fifteenth-century Venetian printers which he first used for printing his own prose romance, *The Story of the Glittering Plain*, in the summer of 1890, and the 'Troy', a bold clear Gothic style which was first used for the Kelmscott edition of Caxton's *Recuyell of the Histories of Troy* in October 1892. A smaller version of the 'Troy' type was used for the Kelmscott edition of the works of Chaucer, which took over three years to produce and was the most ambitious project undertaken by the Press. All the Kelmscott books were printed in limited editions on hand-made paper, and were bound in half-holland or white pigskin.

The Kelmscott Press mark.

T HAS BEEN told that there was once a young man of free kindred and whose name was Hallblithe: he was fair, strong, & not untried in battle; he was of the House of the Raven of old time. ℭ This man loved an exceeding fair damsel called the Hostage, who was of the

William and May Morris with the workers at the Kelmscott Press.

The Story of the Glittering Plain printed by the Kelmscott Press in 1890 in the Golden type, designed by Morris.

Over page: The Kelmscott Chaucer. Morris designed the binding and the typeface, Burne-Jones the 87 woodcut illustrations. It was completed only a few months before Morris's death.

HERE BEGINNETH THE TALES OF CANTER·
BURY AND FIRST THE PROLOGUE THEREOF

WHAN

THAT Aprille with his shoures soote
The droghte of March hath perced to the roote,
And bathed every veyne in swich licour,
Of which vertu engendred is the flour;
Whan Zephirus eek with his swete breeth
Inspired hath in every holt and heeth

The tendre croppes, and the yonge sonne
Hath in the Ram his halfe cours yronne,
And smale foweles maken melodye,
That slepen al the nyght with open eye,
So priketh hem nature in hir corages;
Thanne longen folk to goon on pilgrimages,
And palmeres for to seken straunge strondes,
To ferne halwes, kowthe in sondry londes;
And specially, from every shires ende
Of Engelond, to Caunterbury they wende,
The hooly blisful martir for to seke,
That hem hath holpen whan that they were
seeke.

BIFIL that in that seson on a day,
In Southwerk at the Tabard as
I lay,
Redy to wenden on my pilgrym-
age
To Caunterbury with ful devout
corage,
At nyght were come into that hostelrye
Wel nyne and twenty in a compaignye,
Of sondry folk, by aventure yfalle
In felaweshipe, and pilgrimes were they alle,
That toward Caunterbury wolden ryde.

They were very expensive, but their popularity led other publishers to copy their style. In 1893 Dent brought out a pseudo-Kelmscott edition of the *Morte d'Arthur* with illustrations in the style of Morris by Aubrey Beardsley.

Morris continued to write books as well as to print them. During the last five years of his life he wrote five prose romances: *The Wood Beyond the World, Of Child Christopher and Fair Goldilind* (both published in 1894), *The Well at the World's End* (1896), *The Water of the Wondrous Isle* and *The Sundering Flood* (both published posthumously in 1897). These were all fairy stories set in far-off times and distant lands. In their archaic prose style and their dream-like, almost enchanted quality they resemble the works of J. R. R. Tolkien. They seem curiously remote from the socialist struggle, and rather the work of the 'dreamer of dreams' of *The Earthly Paradise*. Bernard Shaw described them as 'a startling relapse into literary Pre-Raphaelitism'. Perhaps part of the explanation for their distant, detached quality is that they were mostly written in the small hours of the night as Morris wrestled with increasing insomnia.

Although these prose romances, the Kelmscott Press, and the Society for the Protection of Ancient Buildings, on which he was still active, now took up most of Morris's time and energy, he still continued with his designing. During the 1890s he designed ten wallpapers and two chintzes. His last wallpaper, the 'Compton', was

The 'Compton', Morris's last wallpaper design. It was also used for a chintz.

A sketch by Walter Crane of Morris speaking at a May Day Rally in Hyde Park, 1894. Rather curiously, the banner of the Socialist League is waving above him.

designed early in 1896. Most of the firm's wallpapers and textiles were now being designed by his daughter May, and by J. H. Dearle, who had become manager of the Merton Abbey works. Morris's own visits to Merton Abbey became increasingly few and far between. The work of the Press kept him at Hammersmith and he effectively handed over the management of the firm to Dearle and to two brothers, F. and R. Smith, who had been made partners in 1880.

By the mid-1890s Morris was becoming increasingly frail. The strain of his unceasing round of lecturing and speaking at open-air meetings across the country made him look much older than his sixty years. He found writing more and more of an effort, although early in 1895 he resumed work with Eirikr Magnusson on the translation of the *Heimskringla* which they had begun twenty-three years earlier. He still had the energy to campaign vigorously on behalf of his favourite causes. In the summer he went with Philip Webb and others to Epping Forest to look at the tree-felling going on there. He wrote angry letters to the Press about the wanton destruction of the hornbeam thickets among which he had played so happily when a child. He made a final visit to his beloved cathedrals of northern France. On 3 January 1896 he attended the New Year meeting of the Social

Morris's notes for his last lecture, given to the Hammersmith Socialist Society on 5 January 1876.

Democratic Federation and two days later he gave the last of his regular Sunday evening lectures in the coach-house at Hammersmith. The subject was 'One Socialist Party'. At the end of the month, he attended a meeting of the recently formed National Society for Checking the Abuses of Public Advertising and seconded the resolution 'that it is a national interest to protect rural scenery from unnecessary disfigurement and to maintain dignity and propriety in the aspect of our times'. It was his last public speech.

Appropriately, Morris's last trip abroad was to his beloved North. In July and August 1896, he went on a voyage round the Norwegian fjords. It was not a success, as he was too ill to leave the ship. On his return to England he wanted to get back to Kelmscott. He wrote to Jenny:

I am so distressed that I cannot get down to Kelmscott on Saturday; but I am not well, & the doctors will not let me; please my own dear forgive me, for I long to see you with all my heart.

On 8 September Morris dictated the last lines of *The Sundering Flood*. A few days later congestion of the lungs set in, and he abandoned plans to make a selection from the *Border Ballads* and design a Kelmscott Press edition of the *Morte d'Arthur*. On 12 September Cobden-Sanderson noted in his journal:

It is an astonishing spectacle. He sits speechless waiting for the end to come.... Darkness soon will envelop all the familiar scene, the sweet river, England green and grey, Kelmscott, Kelmscott House, the trees . . . the Press, the passage, the Bindery, the light coming in through the windows . . . the old books on the shelves.

Philip Webb and Burne-Jones were with Morris daily. He died on 3 October 1896, at the age of sixty-two. The family doctor declared

Death-bed sketch of Morris, probably by Charles Fairfax Murray, 4 October 1896.

Jane Morris in the Tapestry Room at Kelmscott Manor after her husband's death.

that, 'he died a victim to his enthusiasm for spreading the principles of socialism'. Another doctor remarked, 'the disease was simply being William Morris and having done more work than most ten men'. Two days after his death Wilfrid Scawen Blunt, the poet and publicist, called on Burne-Jones, who told him that:

his interest in life had come to an end with Morris, as all their ideas and plans of work had been together all their lives. . . . Then I went on to Hammersmith. The coffin, a very plain box, lay in the little room downstairs, with a beautiful old embroidered cloth over it and a small wreath of leaves and sad-coloured flowers. It was the room which was his bedroom, and where he died, with his best and favourite books around him.

Morris was buried in a simple ceremony in Kelmscott churchyard. After a six-month holiday in Egypt, his widow sold Kelmscott House in Hammersmith and went to live at Kelmscott Manor with her daughter Jenny. In 1913 she bought the Manor, which until then was

Morris's funeral cart. His coffin was taken by train to Lechlade Station where 'four countrymen in moleskin bore the body to an open hay cart festooned with vines, with alder and with bullrushes and driven by a man who looked coeval with the Anglo-Saxon Chronicle'.

The simple gravestone designed in the Cotswold tradition by Philip Webb. After Morris's death, Webb virtually gave up his architectural practice. He said, 'my coat feels thinner. One would think I had lost a buttress.'

May Morris, Jane Morris, Jenny Morris and Jenny's nurse in the garden of Kelmscott Manor, after Morris's death.

still being rented, and when she died in 1914, May took up residence there and devoted herself to perpetuating her father's memory. She edited his collected works in twenty-four volumes, which were published between 1910 and 1915, followed by two supplementary volumes in 1936. On May's death in 1938, Kelmscott Manor was left to Oxford University, and in 1962 it passed to the Society of Antiquaries, who have restored it and repaired the many fine Morris tapestries and fabrics there.

Morris's influence lived on long after his death and extended to every aspect of life in which he had been involved. He had regarded himself first and foremost as a designer – he had described himself thus on his membership card for the Democratic Federation – and it was in this sphere that his influence was most perceptible and immediate. Long before he died his designs for wallpapers and textiles were being widely copied. In 1885 Arthur Liberty set up a print works near

Block-printing chintzes at Merton Abbey in the 1930s.

Merton Abbey to produce silk and cotton fabrics similar to Morris's for sale in his new West End shop. After his death, large numbers of fabric printers directly plagiarized his designs. Morris & Co. continued to print the originals until it went into liquidation in 1940. The firm's blocks for printing chintzes were then bought by the Carlisle firm of Stead McAlpin, who gave concessions to use them first to the Old Bleach Linen Company and then, in 1959, to Warner & Sons. In 1965 Sanderson & Co. launched their collection of Morris-designed fabrics, produced by screen-printing rather than the block printing method used at Merton Abbey. Sandersons also still produce Morris wallpapers, having acquired the blocks for printing these from Messrs Jeffrey & Co. in 1930.

In the field of typography and book design Morris's influence was considerable. The success of the Kelmscott Press led to a revival in private printing-presses on both sides of the Atlantic. In 1900 Emery

Walker and Cobden-Sanderson founded the Doves Press at Hammersmith, and in 1913 Daniel Updike opened the Merrymount Press in Boston, Massachusetts. Morris's protest against the poor standard of production of most Victorian books prompted commercial printers and publishers to take much more care over design and binding. Wider margins and clearer typefaces were introduced. Although Morris's own designs were too medieval and ornate to have much impact on ordinary book production, they found their way into some publishers' work. The volumes in the Everyman's Library, started by J. M. Dent in 1905, had decorated title pages and end papers which derived directly from Morris's designs.

Morris's writings and lectures on art and design had a profound influence on those who followed him. His call for the revival of the medieval tradition of craftsmanship was one of the main influences behind the foundation of the Arts and Crafts Movement in Britain at the end of the nineteenth century. This movement developed in a way which Morris would almost certainly have profoundly regretted. His disciples attacked machine-production with a blind ferocity that he had never displayed, and cultivated the romantic medievalism which he had given up as a young man. In 1902 C. R. Ashbee, who as a young designer had been much influenced by Morris's writings and lectures, moved his Guild and School of Handicraft from the East End of London to Chipping Camden in the Cotswolds. At the same time another of Morris's disciples, Ernest Gimson, was gathering together a group of students to work with their own hands building medieval cottages in Cotswold villages. This removal of art from the main centres of modern life was not altogether what Morris had preached. Yet he must be held partly accountable for the spread of rather precious craft shops and potteries across the English countryside which was the legacy of at least one side of the Arts and Crafts Movement.

Morris's influence did not, however, stop with the Arts and Crafts Movement. He has been seen as the pioneer of functionalism, and as such the father of the whole modern movement in design. His stress on simplicity, and his dictum 'have nothing in your house except what you know to be useful or believe to be beautiful' did more than anything else to remove from Victorian drawing-rooms the clutter of tasteless bric-à-brac. It provoked such dramatic changes in fashion as that accomplished by Ambrose Heal in 1898 when he stripped his Tottenham Court Road, London, showrooms of heavy Victorian furniture and filled them instead with plain oak pieces. Morris's lectures and writings on design established ordinary domestic architecture and furniture as worthy objects of the artist's imagination. It inspired the work of a group of English architects, of whom C. F. A. Voysey was the most famous, whose achievement in combining functionalism and good design was celebrated in Hermann

Muthesius's classic book *Das Englische Haus* (1905). Curiously, Morris's ideas on design had more influence abroad than they did in Britain. They were taken up particularly by the Scandinavians, and by Henry van de Velde, Otto Wagner and Walter Gropius who were associated with the Bauhaus, the Weimar School of Art in Germany. These Continental architects and designers achieved a marriage of handicraft and standardized machine-production to produce good but cheap furniture. In 1919 the Bauhaus was reorganized along lines of which Morris would have approved, as a combined academy of art and school of practical craftsmanship. It was to be the most important single source of innovations in architecture and design in the twentieth century. Walter Gropius, the creator of the new Bauhaus, traced its origins back to Morris.

With his deep concern about preserving both the urban and the rural landscape, Morris was in many ways the pioneer of the whole environmental movement which has grown up in the twentieth century. The manifesto which he wrote in 1877 for the Society for the Protection of Ancient Buildings, with its reminder that old buildings 'are not in any sense our property to do as we like with them. We are only trustees for those that come after us', has inspired the campaign for conservation which has gone on ever since. The Society itself, which is still going strong, has played a prominent part in this campaign, pioneering the listing of buildings of historic and architectural interest, securing legislation to preserve them, and by its own efforts saving several important buildings including the Assembly Rooms at Bath. It has directly spawned two active conservation societies with specialist interests, the Georgian Group and the Victorian Society, and played a major role in setting up the National Trust, the Council for the Preservation of Rural England, and the Central Council for the Care of Churches. Morris's strictures on pollution and advertising have a distinctly modern ring. He was a strong advocate of clean air legislation, and of a restriction on advertising which encouraged the accumulation of useless goods and defaced the landscape with signs and hoardings. His plea in an article on *How a Factory Might Be*, that 'our factory must make no sordid litter, befoul no water, nor poison the air with smoke' might well come from Ralph Nader or the Friends of the Earth.

In one specific aspect of the environmental movement Morris's influence has been profound. He was one of the originators of the idea of the Garden City – perhaps the most important concept in town-planning in the twentieth century. It derived from his lifelong passion for gardens, and for the simple rural life. In 1874 he wrote to a friend:

Suppose people lived in little country communities among gardens and green fields, so that you could be in the country in five minutes walk, and had few

wants, almost no furniture for instance, and studied the (difficult) arts of enjoying life, and finding out what they really wanted: then I think one might hope civilization had really begun.

Ten years later in his lecture on *Art and Socialism* he reiterated the point: 'There must be abundant garden space in our towns, and our towns must not eat up the fields and natural features of the country.' Significantly it was one of Morris's closest disciples, Raymond Unwin, who shared his socialist ideals and was a regular contributor to *The Commonweal*, who designed the first garden city in England, at Letchworth in 1903. The 'garden' aspect of new towns and the development of the 'Green Belt' policy of restricting building around cities in modern Britain both owe a good deal to Morris's influence.

It is not so easy to assess Morris's influence as a socialist. *The Times* obituary of the prominent British socialist politician and thinker, Anthony Crosland, who died in February 1977, described him as emphasizing 'the William Morris element in British socialism at the expense of the more forbidding strand normally associated with the Webbs. The denial that Labour should, or need, be identified with a "Thou Shalt Not" philosophy formed an important theme of his work.' It is certainly true that there is a life-affirming side to British socialism which stresses the value of fellowship and brotherhood as well as its more austere side which derives from its Nonconformist and Fabian roots. This may well owe something to Morris's influence. But the Labour movement in Britain has preferred to go down the parliamentary and trade unionist road rather than tread the revolutionary socialist path that Morris would have had it travel. There have, of course, been those who have regretted this, and not all of them total sympathizers with Morris's position. In the preface to the 1931 collection of *Fabian Essays*, Bernard Shaw commented of the early days of the British Socialist movement:

When the greatest Socialist of that day, the poet and craftsman William Morris, told the workers that there was no hope for them save in revolution, we said that if that were true there was no hope at all for them, and urged them to save themselves through Parliament, the municipalities, and the franchise.... It is not so certain today, as it seemed in the eighties, that Morris was not right.

In his own age Morris was regarded first and foremost as a poet. It was through his verses rather than his wallpapers that he entered most Victorian drawing-rooms. He was offered the Professorship of Poetry at Oxford University in succession to Matthew Arnold in 1877, and the position of Poet Laureate after the death of Tennyson in 1892, but he declined both honours. His poetic output was vast. It encompassed the collection of short poems in *The Defence of Guenevere*, *The Earthly Paradise* and *Love Is Enough*, his translations of the *Aeneid* and the

Opposite, Walter Crane's *Homage to Morris: Morris and his friends in Elysium*. Morris sits picking flowers in the foreground with the muse of poetry seated behind and (left to right) Swinburne, Browning, Arnold and Tennyson looking on.

Odyssey, his versions of the Icelandic sagas and the long romances written in his later years. Little of it is read today. Perhaps it shows too many signs of the haste in which much of it was composed, on railway journeys between lectures and in the small hours of the morning. The qualities which made Morris's poetry so popular with the Victorians, its archaism and slow rambling style, are not very appealing to modern readers. But it has had an influence on twentieth-century poetry, most notably on the work of W. B. Yeats, who self-consciously modelled his style on that of Morris whom he described as 'the one perfectly happy and fortunate poet of modern time'.

In which of these many roles has Morris made most impact on the world? Perhaps it is simply as a visionary. He may have failed to convince his own generation. They were quite satisfied with shoddy mass-produced goods, and were more interested in receiving higher wages than in helping to build his socialist Utopia. He may only partially have convinced succeeding generations. But this does not detract from the validity of his attack on life in modern industrial society, nor from the nobility of his vision of what it might be:

Civilisation has reduced the workman to such a skinny and pitiful existence, that he scarcely knows how to frame a desire for any life much better than that which he now endures perforce. It is the province of art to set the true ideal of a full and reasonable life before him, a life to which the perception and creation of beauty, the enjoyment of real pleasure that is, shall be felt to be as necessary to man as his daily bread.

Few people have ever tried to live out that ideal more fully than William Morris.

1834 24 March, William born at Elm House, Walthamstow, the third of nine children of William and Emma Morris.

1840 Family moves to Woodford Hall in Epping Forest.

1848 February, starts at Marlborough. Autumn, family moves to Water House, Walthamstow.

1851 Christmas, leaves Marlborough after a riot and continues his education at home.

1853 January, Morris and Burne-Jones start at Exeter College, Oxford. Meet with other undergraduates in Faulkner's rooms and discuss forming a brotherhood.

1854 Summer, first visit abroad, to Belgium and northern France.

1855 March, comes of age and inherits an annual income of £900. July, goes on walking tour of northern France with Burne-Jones and Fulford, and decides to devote himself to art. November, leaves Oxford University.

1856 January, *The Oxford and Cambridge Magazine*; starts work in Street's office in Oxford and meets Philip Webb. August, office moves to London and Morris takes rooms in Bloomsbury with Burne-Jones. November, they move to Rossetti's old rooms in Red Lion Square. December, Morris leaves Street's office.

1857 August, work begins on the Oxford Union frescoes. October, meets Jane Burden.

1858 March, work on frescoes abandoned; *The Defence of Guenevere* published.

1859 April, marries Jane at St Michael's, Oxford.

1860 Late summer; moves into Red House, Bexleyheath.

1861 January, birth of a daughter, Jenny. April, foundation of Morris, Marshall, Faulkner & Co. in Red Lion Square.

1862 March, birth of second daughter, May. Designs his first wallpaper, the 'Trellis'.

1865 November, Morris family and the firm move to Queen Square, Bloomsbury.

1867 June, *The Life and Death of Jason* published.

1868 April, publication of the first part of *The Earthly Paradise*. October, begins studying Norse with Eirikr Magnusson.

1869 January, *The Saga of Gunnlaug Worm Tongue* published.

1870 Publication of *The Volsung Saga* and *A Book of Verse*.

1871 May, joint tenancy of Kelmscott Manor with Rossetti. July to September, first visit to Iceland.

1873 July to September, second visit to Iceland. November, publication of *Love Is Enough*. Family moves to Horrington House, Chiswick.

1875 March, dissolution of the firm and its reconstruction as Morris & Co. November, publication of translation of *The Aeneid*.

1876 October, supports Bulgarian Atrocities campaign. November, elected Treasurer of Eastern Question Association; *Sigurd the Volsung* published.

1877 March, founds Society for the Protection of Ancient Buildings; firm's showrooms move to Oxford Street. December, first public lecture on *The Decorative Arts*.

1878 October, family moves to Kelmscott House, Hammersmith.

1879 Autumn, becomes Treasurer of National Liberal League.

1881 November, resigns from National Liberal League; firm's works move to Merton Abbey.

1882 *Hopes and Fears of Art* published.

1883 January, joins Democratic Federation.

1884 January, publication of *Art and Socialism*. Spring, with Hyndman produces *A Summary of the Principles of Socialism*. December, founds the Socialist League.

1885 Publication of *Useful Work versus Useless Toil*. February, first issue of *The Commonweal*; *Chants for Socialists* published. March, first part of *The Pilgrims of Hope* appears in print.

1886 November, *The Dream of John Ball* begins to appear in *The Commonweal*.

1887 April, first volume of the *Odyssey* published. 13 November, 'Bloody Sunday'.

1888 May, *Signs of Change* published. December, *House of the Wolfings* published.

1889 July, attends Second International in Paris. November, *The Roots of the Mountains* published.

1890 January, first part of *News From Nowhere* published. June, *Story of the Glittering Plain*. November, Hammersmith Branch withdraws from the Socialist League.

1891 January, the Kelmscott Press founded at Hammersmith.

1893 May, *The Manifesto of English Socialists*; *Socialism, its Growth and Outcome* published.

1894 June, *How I Became a Socialist*. August, work starts on Kelmscott Chaucer; *The Wood Beyond the World* and *Of Child Christopher and Fair Goldilind* published.

1896 *The Well at the World's End* published. 3 October, Morris dies at Kelmscott House, Hammersmith; buried in Kelmscott village churchyard.

1897 *The Water of the Wondrous Isle* and *The Sundering Flood* published.

SELECT BIBLIOGRAPHY

The Collected Works of William Morris, edited by May Morris (24 volumes, London 1910–15, new edition New York 1966) provide the most comprehensive source of Morris's own poems, lectures and other writings. They are supplemented by May Morris, *William Morris: Artist, Writer, Socialist* (2 volumes, London 1936). A useful and representative selection from Morris's work, together with photographs of his designs and a valuable essay on his life, can be found in *William Morris: Selected Writings and Designs*, edited by Asa Briggs (London and Baltimore 1962).

The longest, and fullest, biography of Morris is J. W. Mackail's *The Life of William Morris* (2 volumes, London and New York 1899). The best modern biography is undoubtedly Philip Henderson's *William Morris: His Life, Work and Friends* (London and New York 1967) which makes good use of previously unpublished letters. *William Morris: His Life and Work* by Jack Lindsay (London 1975) is an equally readable, though less authoritative and original biography. Paul Thompson's *The Life and Work of William Morris* (London and New York 1967) is good on Morris's interest in architecture and socialism.

The best study of Morris's political ideas and activities, written from an avowedly Marxist standpoint, is E. P. Thompson's *William Morris: Romantic to Revolutionary* (London 1955, New York 1961, revised edition London 1977). Raymond Watkinson's *William Morris as Designer* (London and New York 1967) provides a well illustrated introduction to this aspect of Morris's work, the significance and effects of which are assessed in Nikolaus Pevsner's *Pioneers of Modern Design from William Morris to Walter Gropius* (New York 1957, London 1960). *The Stained Glass of William Morris and his Circle* (New Haven and London 1975) by A. C. Sewter is the standard authority on the subject and well illustrated.

LIST OF ILLUSTRATIONS

'Mr Morris reading poems to Mr Burne-Jones'. Caricature by Burne-Jones. British Museum, London.

22 Three soldiers as aesthetes from *Patience* at the Opéra Comique, London, 1881. By courtesy of the Victoria and Albert Museum, London. Photo Mrs Grygierczyk.

23 Jane Burden, aged 18. Detail of portrait sketch by Rossetti, Oxford, 1858. National Gallery of Ireland, Dublin.

24 *Miss Siddal standing next to an easel.* Drawing by Rossetti. Formerly at Bath, destroyed during the Second World War.

Morris presenting a ring to his future wife. Caricature by Rossetti, 1857. City Museum and Art Gallery, Birmingham.

25 *Queen Guenevere* or *La Belle Iseult.* Oil painting by Morris, 1858. Tate Gallery, London.

26 Charles Faulkner. Nineteenth-century photograph.

27 Red House, Bexleyheath, Kent. Photo National Monuments Record.

Entrance hall of Red House. Photo *Country Life.*

28 Painted tiles in the garden porch of Red House. Photo Dennis Frone.

'Flamma Troiae'. Design by Morris for an embroidered panel, *c.* 1860. Crown copyright. Victoria and Albert Museum, London.

29 Glassware designed by Philip Webb, 1859. Crown copyright.

Victoria and Albert Museum, London.

30 'The Sermon on the Mount'. Design by Rossetti for stained glass. William Morris Gallery, Walthamstow.

Morris in workman's smock. Photograph, 1870s. Photo St Bride Printing Library, London.

31 North-west transept, International Exhibition, South Kensington, London, 1862. Photo Radio Times Hulton Picture Library.

The Medieval Court at the International Exhibition, 1862. Photo Radio Times Hulton Picture Library.

32 'St Paul Preaching at Athens'. Cartoon by Morris and Ford Madox Brown for stained glass, 1862. William Morris Gallery, Walthamstow.

Stained-glass window designed by Morris in Selsley Church, Gloucestershire. Photo Dennis Frone.

33 'King Arthur and Sir Lancelot'. Cartoon by Morris for stained glass. William Morris Gallery, Walthamstow.

Panel painted by Morris on the St George cabinet designed by Philip Webb. Crown copyright. Victoria and Albert Museum, London.

34 Panelled Room in Kelmscott Manor, Oxfordshire. Photo Radio Times Hulton Picture Library.

Victorian interior. Photograph, 1867. Photo Radio Times Hulton Picture Library.

35 The Sussex rush-seated chairs from a Morris and Company catalogue published after Morris's death. William Morris Gallery, Walthamstow.

The 'Morris' reclining chair. William Morris Gallery, Walthamstow.

36 Detail from an earthenware tile panel with nine scenes from *The Sleeping Beauty* story, designed by Burne-Jones, with swan tiles designed by Webb. Crown copyright. Victoria and Albert Museum, London.

Tiles designed for Morris, Marshall, Faulkner & Company by William de Morgan, Burne-Jones and Webb. William Morris Gallery, Walthamstow.

Embroidered panel designed by Morris and worked in silks by Catherine (Mrs Henry) Holiday, *c.* 1877. Crown Copyright. Victoria and Albert Museum, London.

Embroidery designed by Morris, in Kelmscott Manor, Oxfordshire. Photo National Monuments Record.

37 'Trellis' wallpaper designed by Morris, 1862. William Morris Gallery, Walthamstow.

Morris's original design for 'Wild Tulip' wallpaper, *c.* 1884. City Museum and Art Gallery, Birmingham.

'Wild Tulip' wallpaper, 1884. Crown copyright. Victoria and Albert Museum, London.

38 'Fruit' wallpaper, 1864. Crown copyright. Victoria and Albert Museum, London.

39 The Green Dining Room by Morris & Company in the Victoria and Albert Museum. Crown copyright. Victoria and Albert Museum, London.

40 Morris cutting a wood block for *The Earthly Paradise*. Caricature by Burne-Jones. British Museum, London.

41 Title page of *The Earthly Paradise*, 1868.

Burne-Jones wood engraving for *The Earthly Paradise*, cut by Lucy Faulkner. William Morris Gallery, Walthamstow.

42 Dante Gabriel Rossetti. Photograph by Lewis Carroll, October 1863. Gernsheim Collection, University of Texas.

43 Jane Morris posed by Rossetti and photographed by Parsons in the garden of Rossetti's house in Cheyne Walk, 1865. Photo St Bride Printing Library, London.

44 'The M's at Ems'. Caricature by Rossetti. British Museum, London.

45 William Morris. Photograph, 1870s. Photo Radio Times Hulton Picture Library.

46 Garden front of Kelmscott Manor, Oxfordshire. Photo National Monuments Record.

Morris's bedroom, Kelmscott Manor. Photo *Country Life*.

47 *La Pia de' Tolomei*. Oil painting by Rossetti, 1880. Helen Foresman Spencer Museum of Art, University of Kansas.

49 Morris and Burne-Jones in the garden of The Grange, Fulham. Photograph, 1874. Crown copyright. Victoria and Albert Museum, London.

50 Georgiana Burne-Jones. Portrait by Sir Edward Poynter, 1870. Private collection.

Jane Morris. Photograph posed by Rossetti, 1865. Crown copyright. Victoria and Albert Museum, London.

51 The Morris and Burne-Jones families in the garden of The Grange, Fulham. Photograph by Frederick Hollyer, 1874. Crown copyright. Victoria and Albert Museum, London.

The Morris and Burne-Jones children in the garden of The Grange. Photograph by Frederick Hollyer, 1874. National Portrait Gallery, London.

Burne-Jones and Morris at table at The Grange, with Philip Burne-Jones looking on. Caricature by Burne-Jones from *Memorials of Edward Burne-Jones*, 1904.

52 A page of the poem 'Lonely Love and Loveless Death' from *A Book of Verse*, written and decorated by Morris, 1870. Crown copyright. Victoria and Albert Museum, London.

53 Page from the Horace's *Odes* transcribed and decorated by Morris, 1875. Bodleian Library, Oxford.

55 Binding designed by Morris and Philip Webb for *The Story of the Volsungs and Niblungs*, 1870. William Morris Gallery, Walthamstow.

56 Farmhouses and waterfalls near Reykjavik, Iceland. Photo Radio Times Hulton Picture Library.

Morris eating fish in Iceland. Caricature by Burne-Jones from *Memorials of Edward Burne-Jones*, 1904

57 Half-title page from *The Story of Sigurd the Volsung*, with dedication to Algernon Charles Swinburne in Morris's handwriting, 1877. British Museum, London.

'Neutrality under Difficulties'. Cartoon from *Punch*, 5 August 1876. Photo Mansell Collection.

59 William Morris. Photograph, 1880. Photo Mansell Collection.

60 'Rupes Topseia'. Caricature by Rossetti. Members of the Morris firm seated in the background are Faulkner, Rossetti, Burne-Jones, Madox Brown, Webb and Marshall. British Museum, London.

61 'Tulip' chintz, 1875. Crown copyright. Victoria and Albert Museum, London.

62 Chair used by Morris when weaving. William Morris Gallery, Walthamstow.

63 'Lily' Kidderminster carpet designed by Morris, 1877. Crown

copyright. Victoria and Albert Museum, London.

Original design for 'Anemone' machine-woven fabric, 1875. City Museum and Art Gallery, Birmingham.

64 'Hammersmith' carpet designed by Morris for Clouds. Crown copyright. Victoria and Albert Museum, London.

65 Kelmscott House, Hammersmith. Photograph of the exterior, 1880s. Photo Hammersmith Public Library.

'Cabbage and the Vine' tapestry woven by Morris, now in Kelmscott Manor. Courtesy Society of Antiquaries of London.

66 Hand weaving looms at the Morris & Co. workshops, Merton Abbey. Photo William Morris Gallery, Walthamstow.

Dyeing vats at Merton Abbey. William Morris Gallery, Walthamstow.

67 Exterior of the Morris & Co. workshops at Merton Abbey. Photo William Morris Gallery, Walthamstow.

Exterior of the Morris & Co. showroom at 449 Oxford Street, London.

68 Bedford Park, London. Lithograph by F. Hamilton Jackson.

Cover of a Morris & Co. catalogue of upholstered furniture, 1880s. William Morris Gallery, Walthamstow.

Wallpaper design by Morris for Balmoral Castle, 1887. Photo courtesy of E. A. Entwisle.

70 Choir of Christ Church Cathedral, Oxford, before the rebuilding of the east end in 1853. Watercolour. Photo National Monuments Record.

Choir of Christ Church Cathedral, Oxford. Photograph, after 1853. Photo National Monuments Record.

72 Morris giving a lecture on weaving. Caricature by Burne-Jones. William Morris Gallery, Walthamstow.

73 William Morris. Photograph, mid-1880s. Photo Radio Times Hulton Picture Library.

Cover of Morris's pamphlet *Useful Work v. Useless Toil*, 1885.

76 'The unemployed in London: "We've got no work to do".' Illustration from the *Illustrated London News*, 20 February 1886. Photo ILN Picture Library.

Morris's library in Kelmscott House, Hammersmith, photographed by Emery Walker. Photo Hammersmith Public Library.

77 Karl Marx in mid-career. Photo International Instituut voor Socieal Geschiedenis, Amsterdam.

78 Cover of Morris's pamphlet *Monopoly, or How Labour Is Robbed*, 1890.

Democratic Federation' membership card designed by Morris.

79 Cover of *A Summary of the Principles of Socialism*, 1884. Pamphlet written by H. M. Hyndman and Morris.

Cover of *Chants for Socialists* by Morris, 1885.

80 Friedrich Engels. Photograph, c. 1890. Photo Mansell Collection.

Philip Webb. Portrait by C. Fairfax Murray, 1873. National Portrait Gallery, London.

81 May Morris with her husband Henry Halliday Sparling and a Swedish economist, Steffan, and his wife. Photograph. National Portrait Gallery, London.

Eleanor Aveling, daughter of Karl Marx. Photograph, c. 1880. Photo Radio Times Hulton Picture Library.

82 Henry Mayers Hyndman (left) speaking with Rappaport at the International Socialistic Congress at Stuttgart, c. 1907. Photo Radio Times Hulton Picture Library.

Caricature by Burne-Jones, from his account book. Fitzwilliam Museum, Cambridge.

83 The Morning Room at Clouds, near East Knoyle, Wiltshire. Photograph, 1904. Photo *Country Life*.

The Great Parlour, Wightwick Manor, Shropshire. Photo *Country Life*.

85 The Hammersmith Branch of the Socialist League. Photograph. Crown copyright. Victoria and Albert Museum, London.

87 Mob in St James's Street, London, February 1886. Contemporary print.

'The Attitude of the Police', cartoon, 1886. William Morris Gallery, Walthamstow.

88 Riots in Trafalgar Square, London, on Sunday, 13 November 1887. Illustration from the *Illustrated London News*, 19 November 1887.

Cover of pamphlet *Alfred Linnell: A Death Song*, 1887.

92 William Morris. Oil painting by W.B. Richmond, 1880s. National Portrait Gallery, London.

93 'Rossetti's name is heard in America' (Oscar Wilde lecturing). Caricature by Max Beerbohm, from *Rossetti and his Circle*, London, 1922.

94 Interior of the coach-house, Kelmscott House, Hammersmith. Photo William Morris Gallery, Walthamstow.

Annie Besant. Photograph, 1885. Photo Radio Times Hulton Picture Library.

95 Original cast list of *The Tables Turned or, Nupkins Awakened, A Socialist Interlude* by William Morris, as for the first time played at the Hall of the Socialist League on Saturday, 15 October 1887.

97 Illustration for *A Dream of John Ball and a King's Lesson*, 1892. Wood-engraving by Burne-Jones. Photo Eileen Tweedy.

98 Morris and Burne-Jones. Photograph, c. 1890. Photo Hammersmith Public Library.

99 Frontispiece of *News From Nowhere*, published by the Kelmscott Press, 1892.

100 Kelmscott press mark.

101 William Morris, May Morris and workers at the Kelmscott Press. Photograph. Crown copyright. Victoria and Albert Museum, London.

Detail of a page of the Kelmscott Press 1891 edition of *The Story of the Glittering Plain*.

102 Binding designed by Morris for the Kelmscott Press *Chaucer*. William Morris Gallery, Walthamstow.

103 Page of the Kelmscott Press *Chaucer*.

104 'Compton' design for wallpaper and chintz, 1896. William Morris Gallery, Walthamstow.

105 'William Morris speaking from a wagon in Hyde Park, May 1, 1894'. Pen sketch by Walter Crane, from his book *William Morris to Whistler*, 1911.

106 Notes for Morris's last lecture to the Hammersmith Socialist Society, 5 January 1896.

107 Death-bed sketch of Morris, probably by Charles Fairfax Murray (also attributed to W.B. Richmond), 4 October 1896. Photo Hammersmith Public Library.

108 Jane Morris in the Tapestry Room, Kelmscott Manor, after Morris's death. Photo St Bride Printing Library, London.

109 Morris's funeral cart. Photograph, 1896. Photo William Morris Gallery, Walthamstow.

Morris's grave in Kelmscott churchyard. Drawing. William Morris Gallery, Walthamstow.

110 May Morris, Jane Morris, Jenny Morris and Jenny's nurse in the garden of Kelmscott Manor, after Morris's death. Photo William Morris Gallery, Walthamstow.

111 Block-printing chintzes at Merton Abbey. Photograph, 1930s. Photo William Morris Gallery, Walthamstow.

114 *Homage to Morris: Morris and his friends in Elysium*. Drawing by Walter Crane. William Morris Gallery, Walthamstow.

WHERE TO SEE MORRIS'S WORK

Red House, Bexleyheath, still has much of its original furniture and decoration. It is open for visiting at certain times by appointment with the present owner, Mr Edward Hollamby.

Kelmscott Manor, near Lechlade, Oxfordshire, contains many works of art by Morris and his circle. It is now owned by the Society of Antiquaries and is open to the public on six advertised days in the year and at other times by appointment with the tenant.

Kelmscott House, 26 Upper Mall, London W6, is the headquarters of the William Morris Society who hold regular meetings and are building up a collection of Morrisiana.

The William Morris Gallery, Forest Road, London E17, housed in Water House, the Morris's home from 1848 to 1856, has the most comprehensive collection of Morris's designs and works of art as well as many relics of his life. It is open on weekdays from 10 a.m. to 5 p.m. and on the first Sunday of every month.

The Victoria and Albert Museum, London, has a display of furniture and textiles by Morris as well as containing the Green Dining Room. Wightwick Manor, three miles west of Wolverhampton and now the property of the National Trust, is the best example of a private house decorated by Morris & Co.

All Saints Church, Selsley, Gloucestershire; St Martin's Church, Scarborough, Yorkshire; All Saints Church, Middleton Cheney, Northamptonshire; St Michael's Church, Brighton, and Christ Church Cathedral, Oxford, have particularly good stained-glass windows by Morris.

INDEX

Page numbers in italic indicate illustrations